Crafting Applications with ChatGPT API

Using Python

Mike Gold

Crafting Applications with ChatGPT API

Using Python

Mike Gold

ISBN 979-8-89121-043-1

Leanpub

This is a Leanpub book. Leanpub empowers authors and publishers with the Lean Publishing process. Lean Publishing is the act of publishing an in-progress ebook using lightweight tools and many iterations to get reader feedback, pivot until you have the right book and build traction once you do.

Dedicated to my wife: Editor, Mother, and Best Friend

Contents

What is ChatGPT and Why Use It?

Introduction

In the realm of technology, few innovations have sparked as much excitement and potential as ChatGPT. Imagine a world where machines not only understand us but also assist us in crafting imaginative stories, bridging language barriers, and inventing delicious recipes. This book is your gateway to unlocking the remarkable capabilities of ChatGPT. We will embark on a journey that transforms familiar territory into a playground with infinite possiblities using three extraordinary applications.

Buckle up as we accelerate towards untapped creativity and functionality, harnessing the synergy of imagination, code, and possibility. In the chapters that follow, you'll witness the awesome impact of cutting-edge artificial intelligence on the practicalities of application development. We'll begin by producing colorful conversations between animals in a desktop application, then discover how to translate language seamlessly, and finish with instantaneous recipes using the ingredients you have on hand through a web app. This book is your compass through this landscape of innovation.

Join us at the intersection of imagination and technology, where the ChatGPT API transforms bold ideas into tangible realities. Whether you're a seasoned developer seeking to push the boundaries of what's possible or an enthusiast curious about the future of AI-driven applications, this thrilling expedition promises to reshape how we interact with computers and the possibilities that lie ahead. Get ready to witness the dawn of a new era in application development with ChatGPT as your guide and inspiration.

In this opening chapter, we uncover the essence of ChatGPT and explore the compelling reasons behind its utilization in various domains.

Background of ChatGPT

At the forefront of modern artificial intelligence, the Generative pre-trained Transformer, or GPT, has emerged as a monumental breakthrough. Developed by OpenAI, a pioneering research organization, GPT represents a culmination of years of research and innovation in natural language processing (NLP). The GPT series of models are designed to understand and generate human-like text, effectively bridging the gap between human communication and machine comprehension.

OpenAI, a trailblazing institution founded in 2015, stands as a beacon of ingenuity in the AI landscape. Committed to advancing artificial intelligence for the betterment of humanity, OpenAI has consistently pushed the boundaries of what AI can achieve. GPT, which stands for "Generative Pre-trained Transformer," is one of OpenAI's flagship innovations, with multiple iterations each building upon the successes of its predecessors. These models are characterized by their remarkable ability to generate coherent and contextually relevant text, fundamentally transforming how machines process and produce language. The democratization of AI knowledge through research papers, tools, and APIs, including the much-acclaimed ChatGPT API, showcases OpenAI's dedication to enabling developers, researchers, and enthusiasts to harness the power of AI in ways that were once relegated to the realm of science fiction.

Benefits and Use Cases

The allure of ChatGPT transcends its technical intricacies, as it offers a plethora of tangible benefits across diverse applications. Below are some of the ways people are leveraging the power of Natural Language processing through OpenAI's brainchild.

Customer Support and Service: Companies are leveraging Chat-GPT to revolutionize their customer support systems. From responding to queries and troubleshooting to guiding users through complex processes, ChatGPT is reshaping customer service interactions.

Content Generation and Marketing: In the realm of content creation and marketing, ChatGPT proves to be an invaluable tool. It assists in generating captivating blog posts, social media content, and marketing copy, freeing up creative resources and accelerating content production.

Programming and Coding: Within the landscape of artificial intelligence and programming, ChatGPT emerges as a valuable tool with the potential to revolutionize coding practices. By seamlessly blending AI capabilities with coding tasks, ChatGPT offers developers an array of advantages. It can assist in tasks ranging from code composition and elucidating intricate programming concepts to offering resolutions for coding hurdles. In doing so, ChatGPT caters to both neophyte and proficient programmers, fostering an environment of enhanced productivity and knowledge dissemination.

Idea Brainstorming: ChatGPT's role in brainstorming lies in its ability to foster creativity and broaden horizons. By leveraging its language generation capabilities, the API can inspire unique ideas that might not have emerged through traditional methods. It can introduce unconventional viewpoints and challenge established thought patterns, enriching your ideation process. Furthermore, whether you're conceptualizing a new storyline, envisioning a visual masterpiece, devising strategic business moves, or revolutionizing industries with groundbreaking innovations, ChatGPT's adaptable insights can provide valuable inputs across these diverse domains. Integrating ChatGPT into your brainstorming endeavors empowers you to leverage AI-driven creativity to its fullest potential.

Language Learning and Practice: ChatGPT serves as a versatile language partner, possessing the capability to enhance vocabulary, correct grammar, and facilitate interactive language practice. This makes it suitable for learners of all proficiency levels.

Who is this Book For?

This book is crafted for the curious minds eager to harness the transformative power of AI in everyday applications. Whether you're a budding developer aiming to integrate ChatGPT into your projects, a tech enthusiast wanting to grasp the practicality of artificial intelligence, or simply someone fascinated by the blend of technology and imagination, this guide offers insights that cater to all. Dive into a world where stories come alive, languages intertwine seamlessly, and recipes emerge from mere ingredients. No prior expertise in AI is required, just an enthusiasm to explore its boundless potential. With the hundreds of possibilities for innovation that ChatGPT offers, there's no need to delay any longer. Let's dive right into our first application: a Python-based storytelling platform.

Animal Chat

Figure 1. Tea Party

Our initial application is designed with simplicity in mind. We'll start by selecting two animals from the two drop down menus. Then we'll be prompted to provide a scenario for the dialogue. This can be anything we envision, such as the two animals engaged in a heated debate over the responsibility of taking out the garbage.

Where to begin

We'll start by preparing the foundational tools for our project. First, we'll walk you through the steps of setting up Python, the programming language that forms the backbone of our application. Next, we'll guide you through the process of installing the OpenAI library, which is essential for integrating ChatGPT's capabilities into our application.

Setting up Python

Before we dive into our application, ensure that Python is properly set up on your machine. We'll provide step-by-step instructions for installing Python, along with any necessary dependencies, so you can start coding without any hiccups.

Step 1: Download Python

Open a web browser and navigate to the official Python website: https://www.python.org/

On the main page, find the "Downloads" tab. Click on it.

Step 2: Choose the Python Version

On the download page, find the latest versions of Python. There might be two available—Python 2.x and Python 3.x. We recommend Python 3.x, as Python 2.x is no longer actively maintained.

Step 3: Download Installer

Scroll down to find the version you want to install (e.g., Python 3.8, Python 3.9). Depending on your operating system (Windows, macOS, or Linux), click on the appropriate download link.

Step 4: Run Installer

Locate the downloaded installer file (it should have a .exe extension on Windows or .pkg on macOS). Double-click the installer to run it.

Step 5: Configure Installation

In the installation window we have various options. Ensure the **"Add Python x.x to PATH"** option is checked. This will make it easier to run Python from the command line. We can customize the installation directory if needed, or just leave it as the default.

Click the "**Install Now**" button to begin the installation process.

Step 6: Installation Complete

Once the installation is complete, we'll see a screen indicating that Python was installed successfully.

We will now close the installer.

Step 7: Verify Installation

Open a command prompt (Windows) or terminal (macOS/Linux). Type:

```
1    python --version
```

and press Enter. We can see the version number that we installed (e.g., Python 3.11.4). Congratulations, Python is now installed! We're ready to start coding in Python, utilizing its powerful capabilities.

Installing the OpenAI library

To tap into the power of ChatGPT, we'll need to integrate the OpenAI library into our project. We'll guide you through the process of installing the library and setting up the necessary authentication, enabling seamless communication with the ChatGPT API. By the end of this section, we'll be equipped with the tools needed to leverage ChatGPT's language generation capabilities into the storytelling application.

Installing the OpenAI library in Python is a straightforward process. Here's how to do it:

Step 1: Open a Terminal or Command Prompt

For Windows: Press the Windows key, search for "Command Prompt," and open it. For macOS and Linux: Open the Terminal application.

Step 2: Use pip to Install the OpenAI Library

In the Terminal or Command Prompt, type the following command:

```
1   pip install openai
```

and press Enter to install the OpenAI library using pip, which is Python's package manager. To test if it installed correctly, simply type into the command prompt:

```
1    python
```

and at the python >>> prompt, type:

```
1   import openai
```

If you don't get an error, openai was installed correctly.

Type ctrl-Z to exit python.

Designing the UI

First, we'll focus on the user interface (UI) of our storytelling application. A user-friendly and visually appealing interface is crucial for a positive user experience. We'll explore the Tkinter library, a popular choice for creating graphical user interfaces in Python.

Introducing Tkinter for GUI

Tkinter provides a simple yet powerful way to create interactive GUI applications. We'll introduce the basics of Tkinter, setting up a window, adding widgets, and handling user interactions. By the end of this section, we'll have a solid understanding of Tkinter's capabilities and how to utilize them for our project.

installing Tkinter

To install TkInter for Python, simply type the following command into the Command Prompt and hit enter:

```
1   pip install tk
```

Now we are ready to create a dialog with user input and a few components in Tk.

Creating the UI

To facilitate user interaction, we'll implement dropdown menus that allow users to select their preferred animals. We'll also guide you through the process of incorporating input fields where users can define the context of the animal dialogue. By combining these elements, we'll be laying the foundation for a user-friendly interface that enables users to customize their storytelling experience.

Creating the Main Window

Now we need to import the Tk library to get access to the UI components of tickle:

```
1   # import toolkit
2   import tkinter as tk
3   # import the toolkit interface
4   from tkinter import ttk
```

We are now ready to set up the application. In toolkit, that means constructing the toolkit app and running an event loop. The event loop is what keeps the application running and responsive to user interactions, such as button clicks. It will keep the "Animal Discussion Scenario" window open until the user decides to close it.

```
1   import tkinter as tk
2   from tkinter import ttk
3
4   app = tk.Tk()
5   app.title("Animal Discussion Scenario")
6   app.mainloop()  # event loop
```

This code will bring up a blank window until we fill in its contents:

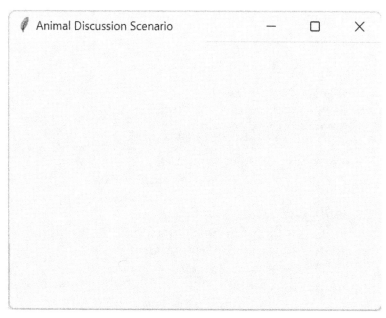

Figure 2. Blank Tk Window

Filling in the UI Code

Having established our main window, it's time to design the inner components of our UI. For animal selections, we're creating two dropdown lists populated with various animal names. Additionally, we're providing a text input field where users can draft a hypothetical dialogue between the animals. To finalize the user's choices, a 'Submit' button is included. Clicking submit will display the user's selections. Later in this chapter we'll discuss integration with the OpenAI library. Note that each component (label, combobox, text, and button) all have a grid method that helps us to lay out the UI controls.

```
1   import tkinter as tk
2   from tkinter import ttk
3
4   def submit():
5       animal1 = combo1.get()
6       animal2 = combo2.get()
7       scenario = entry_box.get()
8
9       result_text.delete(1.0, tk.END) # Clear any
10                                      # previous
11                                      # results
12      result_text.insert(tk.END, f"Animal 1:
13                          {animal1}\n")
14      result_text.insert(tk.END, f"Animal 2:
15                          {animal2}\n")
16      result_text.insert(tk.END,
17                          f"Discussion scenario:
18                          {scenario}\n")
19
20  app = tk.Tk()
21  app.title("Animal Discussion Scenario")
22
23  # Label and ComboBox for the first animal
24  label1 = ttk.Label(app, text="Select Animal 1:")
25  label1.grid(column=0, row=0, padx=10, pady=5)
26  combo1 = ttk.Combobox(app, values=["Lion",
27    "Elephant","Giraffe", "Kangaroo", "Panda"])
28  combo1.grid(column=1, row=0, padx=10, pady=5)
29  combo1.set("Lion")
30
31  # Label and ComboBox for the second animal
32  label2 = ttk.Label(app, text="Select Animal 2:")
33  label2.grid(column=0, row=1, padx=10, pady=5)
34  combo2 = ttk.Combobox(app, values=["Lion",
35    "Elephant", "Giraffe", "Kangaroo", "Panda"])
```

```
36   combo2.grid(column=1, row=1, padx=10, pady=5)
37   combo2.set("Elephant")
38
39   # Label and Entry for entering the discussion scenario
40   label3 = ttk.Label(app, text=
41                      "Enter Discussion Scenario:")
42   label3.grid(column=0, row=2, padx=10, pady=5)
43   entry_box = ttk.Entry(app, width=30)
44   entry_box.grid(column=1, row=2, padx=10, pady=5)
45
46   # Button to submit the details
47   submit_btn = ttk.Button(app, text="Submit",
48       command=submit)
49   submit_btn.grid(column=1, row=3, padx=10, pady=20)
50
51   # Text widget to display results
52   result_text = tk.Text(app, width=40, height=10)
53   result_text.grid(column=0, row=4, columnspan=2,
54       padx=10, pady=10)
55
56   app.mainloop()
```

Running the Application

Running the code we created will display the storytelling window. Let's try it out! First create a new Python file called StoryTelling.py and paste the code above into it. Then run in the Terminal window.

```
1   python -m StoryTelling
```

This will bring up the application and automatically display the default animals, Lion and Elephant, in the dropdowns:

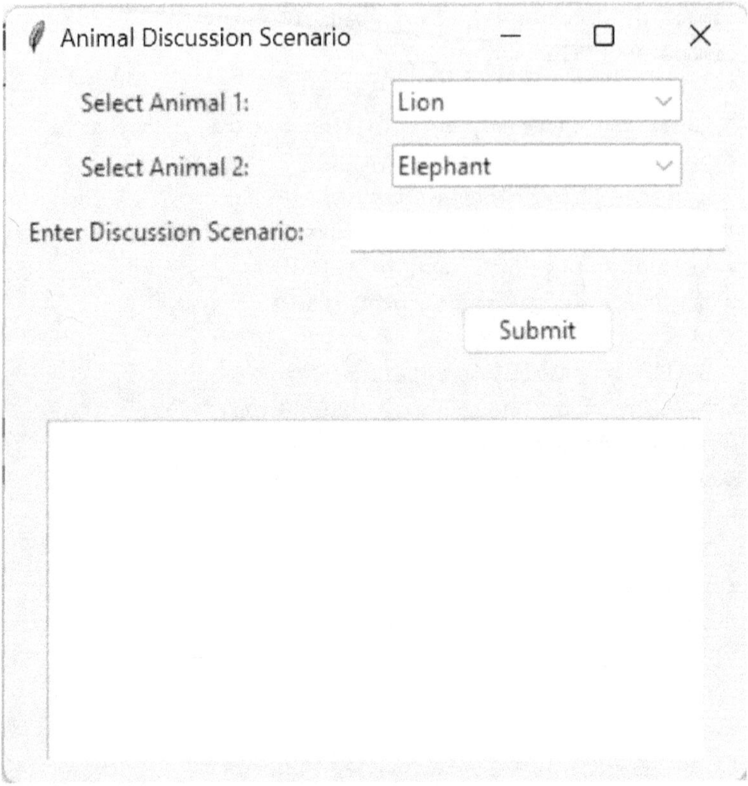

Figure 3. Initial App Screen

Let's type in a scenario for the Lion and Elephant and click the submit button:

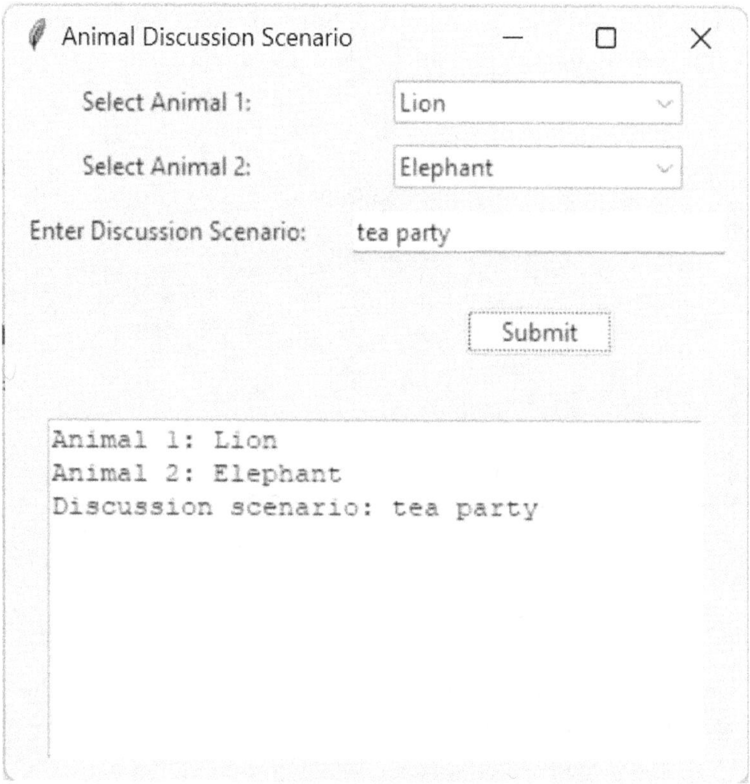

Figure 4. After Submit

Clicking submit displays the choices we made in the result text box we created. Now we are ready to take the next step and integrate OpenAI.

Obtaining an API Key

In order to integrate OpenAI into our application, we are going to need permission to call the OpenAI API. We get permission by using an API Key which we generate from the Open AI site[1]. Go

---

[1] https://openai.com/

to the Open AI page and click **Get Started**. We'll need to register
with them in order to get an API key. Once registered and logged
in, click on the API section:

Figure 5. **Logged in to ChatGPT**

Once registered, we'll notice a dropdown in the upper right hand
corner of our browser. Here is where we can generate or view
existing keys:

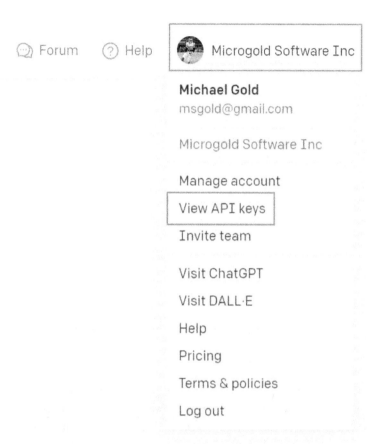

Figure 6. View API Keys

When we click on View API keys, we'll see the following screen which will allow us to generate an API key:

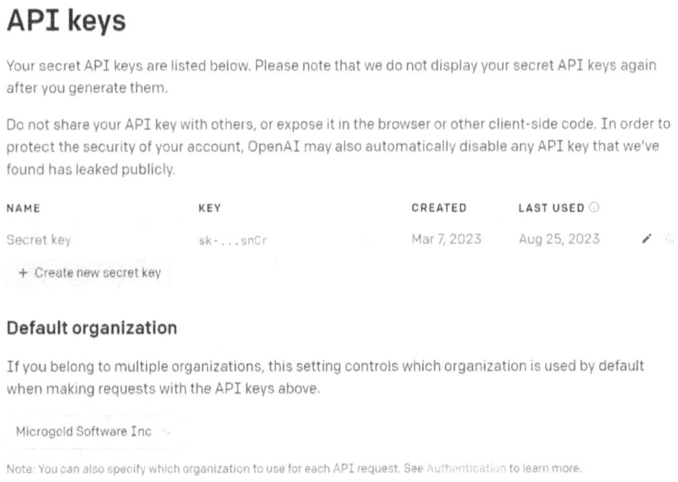

API keys

Your secret API keys are listed below. Please note that we do not display your secret API keys again after you generate them.

Do not share your API key with others, or expose it in the browser or other client-side code. In order to protect the security of your account, OpenAI may also automatically disable any API key that we've found has leaked publicly.

NAME	KEY	CREATED	LAST USED ⓘ	
Secret key	sk-...snCr	Mar 7, 2023	Aug 25, 2023	✎ 🗑

+ Create new secret key

Default organization

If you belong to multiple organizations, this setting controls which organization is used by default when making requests with the API keys above.

Microgold Software Inc ⌄

Note: You can also specify which organization to use for each API request. See Authentication to learn more.

Figure 7. Key Generation

We may also be able to get to the API key screen directly[2] once logged in.

Note: Securely store a backup of the key and keep it confidential. Each API call incurs a cost. The charge varies based on the language model we use. For instance, as of this publication, invoking the GPT-3.5 Turbo model costs $0.002 per call. We can protect ourselves from exploding charges by providing usage limits[3] on our account.

---

[2] https://platform.openai.com/account/api-keys
[3] https://platform.openai.com/account/billing/limits

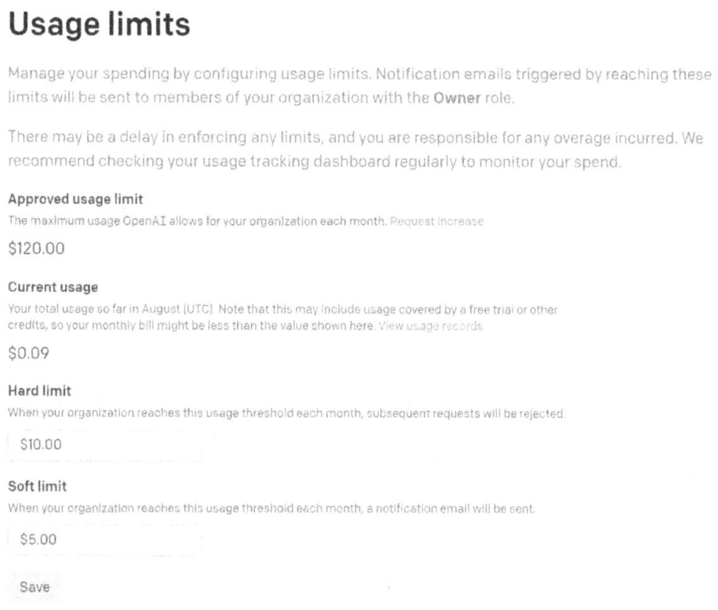

Usage limits

Manage your spending by configuring usage limits. Notification emails triggered by reaching these limits will be sent to members of your organization with the **Owner** role.

There may be a delay in enforcing any limits, and you are responsible for any overage incurred. We recommend checking your usage tracking dashboard regularly to monitor your spend.

Approved usage limit
The maximum usage OpenAI allows for your organization each month. Request increase

$120.00

Current usage
Your total usage so far in August (UTC). Note that this may include usage covered by a free trial or other credits, so your monthly bill might be less than the value shown here. View usage records

$0.09

Hard limit
When your organization reaches this usage threshold each month, subsequent requests will be rejected.

$10.00

Soft limit
When your organization reaches this usage threshold each month, a notification email will be sent.

$5.00

Save

Figure 8. Usage Limits

Integrating OpenAI

Now that we've got a framework for creating our animal storytelling application and the authorization to call OpenAI, let's create a fun application in which two animals chat about any topic we choose. Because we are running Python on our desktop, it's okay to expose the key for the purpose of this application, at least initially. Then we'll show you a way to hide it!

For now, let's add the import for opening OpenAI and assign it our new key:

```
1   import openai
2
3   # assign your api key
4   openai.api_key = '<place your key here>'
```

Let's modify the submit function to invoke ChatGPT and retrieve a
response based on a prompt. This is where the real excitement lies.
We'll ask ChatGPT API to create a dynamic dialogue between two
animals—-an elephant and a lion— at a tea party. The primary task
is to craft the appropriate prompt which we'll derive from the input
parameters of the two animals and the desired interaction scenario.
In the code below, we utilize the OpenAI library to request a chat
completion for our animal dialogue. We generate the prompt from
user input and subsequently add it to the messages collection for
ChatGPT to process.

Once we've called the ChatCompletion function on OpenAI, it will
return a response when it's done processing (this could take a few
seconds). Upon receiving the response, we add it to the result_text
Tk component.

```
1   # form the prompt out of the input inside submit
2   def submit():
3       animal1 = combo1.get()
4       animal2 = combo2.get()
5       scenario = entry_box.get()
6
7       prompt = f"Create a play between a
8         {animal1} and a {animal2} with
9         10 lines of dialog with each animal
10        taking turns to speak. Here is the
11        scenario in which they
12        will engage: {scenario}\n"
13
14      messages = [{'role': 'user', 'content': prompt}]
15
```

```
16      response = openai.ChatCompletion.create(
17          model="gpt-3.5-turbo",
18          messages=messages,
19          temperature=0.8,
20          top_p=1.0,
21          frequency_penalty=0.0,
22          presence_penalty=0.6,
23      )
24
25      chatGPTAnswer =
26          response["choices"][0]["message"]
27                              ["content"]
28      print(chatGPTAnswer)
29      # make result_text scrollable
30
31      result_text.config(state="normal")
32      result_text.delete(1.0, tk.END)  # Clear any
33                                       # previous
34                                       # results
35      result_text.insert(tk.END, chatGPTAnswer)
36      result_text.config(state="disabled")
```

A few things worth noting are some of the parameters of the OpenAPI call and what they mean. Feel free to tweak these parameters to get different flavors of results.

model: Specifies which model to use. In this case, "gpt-3.5-turbo" indicates that you're using the GPT-3.5 Turbo version of the model.

messages: A list of message objects that simulate a conversation. Each message has a 'role' (which can be 'system', 'user', or 'assistant') and 'content' (the content of the message). The model reads the messages in order and generates a continuation. In this instance, the prompt is being formatted as a user message.

temperature: Influences the randomness of the model's responses. A higher value like 1.0 makes output more random, while a lower value like 0.1 makes it more deterministic. In this case, 0.8 is a balance, allowing for some creativity without being too random.

top_p: Also known as nucleus sampling, it's used for controlling randomness. A value of 1.0 means all tokens are considered when generating the response. Lower values (e.g., 0.9) make the outputs more focused and less random by only sampling the most probable tokens.

frequency_penalty: Adjusts the likelihood of tokens based on their frequency. A positive value makes the model more likely to use frequent tokens,while a negative value makes it less likely. At 0.0, there's no penalty applied based on frequency.

presence_penalty: Adjusts the likelihood of tokens based on their presence in the context. A positive value encourages the model to use new tokens, while a negative value discourages the model from introducing new concepts. Here, 0.6 encourages the introduction of new tokens to some extent.

Let's run the application using:

```
1   python -m StoryTelling.py
```

A dialog will appear like the one we created. Let's leave the Lion and Elephant selected and choose a scenario of **tea party**. Click submit and wait a few seconds. You should see the following appear in the bottom text:

Figure 9. tea party dialog

Here is the full dialog between the Elephant and the Lion that was generated.

Dialog between an Elephant and a Lion

Lion: Good afternoon, Elephant! What a splendid tea party
this is.

Elephant: Indeed, Lion! The flowers and the delicious
treats make it such a delightful affair.

Lion: I must say, your elegant presence adds an air of
grandeur to our gathering.

Elephant: Why, thank you, Lion! Your regal mane and
graceful stride make you quite the host.

Lion: Please, do help yourself to some tea and
biscuits. They're fit for royalty, just like
ourselves.

Elephant: How kind of you, Lion. I shall savor every
sip and bite with pleasure.

Lion: Tell me, Elephant, have you ever attended a
tea party before?

Elephant: Surprisingly, this is my first one, Lion.
It's a charming experience, indeed.

Lion: Well, my dear Elephant, I must say you are a
natural at this tea party business.

Elephant: Thank you, Lion. Your hospitality and
company make it all the more enjoyable.

Lion: It is my pleasure, Elephant. Let's continue
to indulge in this enchanting tea party together.

Of course we can adjust the scenario however we want. Let's have
the elephant accidently spill some tea on the lions lap.

Figure 10. Spilled Tea

Below are ChatGPT's fully generated lines including the spilling mishap:

```
 1   Lion: Ah, what a delightful tea party this is!
 2
 3   Elephant: Indeed, the ambiance is quite charming.
 4
 5   Lion: Careful not to spill your tea, Elephant.
 6
 7   Elephant: Fear not, Lion, my trunk ensures a steady grip.
 8
 9   Lion: I'm glad to hear it. This tea is exquisite, don't
10   you think?
11
12   Elephant: Absolutely, Lion. The blend is simply divine.
13
14   Lion: Oh no! My apologies, Elephant, I've spilled tea
15   on your lap.
16
17   Elephant: No worries, Lion. Accidents happen, it's
18   just a little tea.
19
20   Lion: Still, I feel terrible. Allow me to clean it up
21   for you.
22
23   Elephant: That won't be necessary, Lion. It was an
24   innocent mistake.
25
26   Lion: Thank you for being so understanding, Elephant.
27   You truly are a gracious friend.
```

I thought it was a clever twist that the Lion warned the Elephant not to spill his tea, but then spilled his own...on the Elephant!

Scrolling

Another thing we need to add to the UI is the ability for the results to scroll vertically so the user can read the full play. We start by adding a scrollbar widget to our app:

```
1   scrollbar = tk.Scrollbar(app)
```

Now we need to place our scrollbar in the grid layout we've defined

```
1   scrollbar.grid(row=4, column=3, sticky='ns')
```

The Scrollbar widget is placed in the app widget's grid layout at row 4 and column 3. The sticky='ns' argument ensures the scrollbar stretches vertically to fill its assigned grid cell.

Next, when we construct the result_text, we need to have the vertical movement of the result_text widget's content linked to the y-position of the scrollbar :

```
1   result_text = tk.Text(app, width=40, height=10,
2       wrap=tk.WORD, yscrollcommand=scrollbar.set)
```

Finally, we link the scrollbar's motion back to the updating of the result_view's rendered content.

```
1   scrollbar.config(command=result_text.yview)
```

You may be wondering why we need to add both dependencies: One for the scrollbar in the Text widget and one for the Text widget in the scrollbar? We actually do need both linkages and here is why:

The first linkage yscrollcommand=scrollbar.set adjusts the scrollbar based on the content inside the Text widget.

The second linkage scrollbar.config(command=result_text.yview) ensures that the actual movement of the scrollbar scrolls the content in the Text widget.

Both are essential for a fully synchronized, two-way interaction between the scrollbar and the Text widget. If we omit one of them, we'll only have half of the desired behavior.

Here is the full setup code for the widgets including the scrollbar:

```
1   app = tk.Tk()
2   app.title("Animal Discussion Scenario")
3   # Label and ComboBox for the first animal
4   label1 = ttk.Label(app, text="Select Animal 1:")
5   label1.grid(column=0, row=0, padx=10, pady=5)
6   combo1 = ttk.Combobox(app, values=["Lion", "Elephant",
7              "Giraffe", "Kangaroo", "Panda"])
8   combo1.grid(column=1, row=0, padx=10, pady=5)
9   combo1.set("Lion")
10
11  # Label and ComboBox for the second animal
12  label2 = ttk.Label(app, text="Select Animal 2:")
13  label2.grid(column=0, row=1, padx=10, pady=5)
14  combo2 = ttk.Combobox(app, values=["Lion",
15      "Elephant", "Giraffe", "Kangaroo", "Panda"])
16  combo2.grid(column=1, row=1, padx=10, pady=5)
17  combo2.set("Elephant")
18
19  # Label and Entry for entering the discussion scenario
20  label3 = ttk.Label(app, text=
21                      "Enter Discussion Scenario:")
22  label3.grid(column=0, row=2, padx=10, pady=5)
23  entry_box = ttk.Entry(app, width=30)
24  entry_box.grid(column=1, row=2, padx=10, pady=5)
25
26  # Button to submit the details
27  submit_btn = ttk.Button(app, text="Submit",
28     command=submit)
29  submit_btn.grid(column=1, row=3, padx=10, pady=20)
30
31  # make it scrollable
32  # Create a Scrollbar widget
33  scrollbar = tk.Scrollbar(app)
34  scrollbar.grid(row=4, column=3, sticky='ns')
35
```

```
36  # Text widget to display results
37  result_text = tk.Text(app, width=40, height=10,
38      wrap=tk.WORD, yscrollcommand=scrollbar.set)
39  result_text.grid(column=0, row=4, columnspan=2,
40      padx=10, pady=10)
41  result_text.config(state="disabled")
42  # result_text.pack(expand=True, fill=tk.BOTH)
43
44  scrollbar.config(command=result_text.yview)
45
46  app.mainloop()
```

It's exciting to have generated an entire story with the push of a button, but what if we could also generate illustrations for our story at the push of a button?

Generating an Image

The OpenAI library allows us to leverage DALLE-2 to generate either a 128x128, 256x256, or 1024x1024 image from a prompt. For our example, we will be generating a 256x256 image for our story using the input from the user to form the prompt.

Let's start by installing the necessary Python libraries to display the image. For our storytelling app, we'll need libraries that have the ability to retrieve image data from a URL and display it within our label. We'll utilize the requests library to access the URL and obtain our data, and the Pillow library to render that response into an image

```
1    pip install Pillow requests
```

Having installed the required libraries, we can now use them to obtain our image.

```
1  import openai
2  import requests
3  from PIL import Image, ImageTk
```

First, Let's add a new Tk label control to the app to hold our image in the control set up area:

```
1  image_holder = tk.Label(app)
2  image_holder.grid(column=0, row=5, columnspan=4,
3                    padx=10, pady=10)
```

Next, let's create a Python function that employs the OpenAI API, specifically the Image.create function, to produce the image from our prompt. For this task, we'll employ the image-alpha-001 model.

```
1   def generateImage(animal1, animal2, scenario):
2     response = openai.Image.create(
3       model="image-alpha-001",
4       prompt=f"cartoon image of a
5               {animal1} and a {animal2}
6               discussing {scenario}",
7       n=1,   # Number of images to generate
8       size="256x256",   # Size of the generated
9                         # image
10      response_format="url" # Format in which the
11                            # image will be
12                            # received
13    )
14
15    image_url = response.data[0]["url"]
16    return image_url
```

Displaying the Image

The response to our generateImage function gives us the image url we need in order to display our story image. Let's create a new function **display_image_from_url**, that takes the image url generated by DALLE-2 and the Tk label for holding the image as parameters. The function will do two things: it will make a request to the url to get the data, and it will place the returned data from the http response into an image format displayable by our Tk library.

```
1  def display_image_from_url(image_holder, url):
2      # Fetch the image from the URL
3      response = requests.get(url)
4      image_data = BytesIO(response.content)
5
6      # Open and display the image
7      # using PIL and tkinter
8      image = Image.open(image_data)
9      photo = ImageTk.PhotoImage(image)
10
11     # Display the image in the label control
12     update_label_with_new_image(image_holder,
13                                        photo)
```

Once we have an actual image, we can update our label with the image to show in our UI:

```
1  def update_label_with_new_image(label, photo):
2      label.config(image=photo)
3      label.image = photo  # Keep a reference
4                           # to avoid
5                           # garbage collection
```

The only remaining task is to modify the submit function to call our image generating function and image display function:

```
1   def submit():
2       animal1 = combo1.get()
3       animal2 = combo2.get()
4       scenario = entry_box.get()
5
6       prompt = f"Create a play between a
7           {animal1} and a {animal2}
8           with 10 lines of dialog with each animal
9           taking turns to speak. Leave a vertical
10          space between lines after each animal
11          speaks.
12          Here is the scenario in which
13          they will engage: {scenario}\n"
14      messages = [{'role': 'user',
15                   'content': prompt}]
16      response = openai.ChatCompletion.create(
17          model="gpt-3.5-turbo",
18          messages=messages,
19          temperature=0.8,
20          top_p=1.0,
21          frequency_penalty=0.0,
22          presence_penalty=0.6,
23      )
24
25      chatGPTAnswer =  response["choices"][0]
26                          ["message"]["content"]
27      print(chatGPTAnswer)
28
29
30      result_text.config(state="normal")
31      result_text.delete(1.0, tk.END)  # Clear any
32                                       # previous
33                                       # results
34      result_text.insert(tk.END, chatGPTAnswer)
35      result_text.config(state="disabled")
```

```
36
37    image_url = generateImage(animal1, animal2,
38                              scenario)
39    display_image_from_url(image_holder,
40                           image_url)
```

After all is said and done, once we click the submit button with our tea party parameters, we should see something like the following:

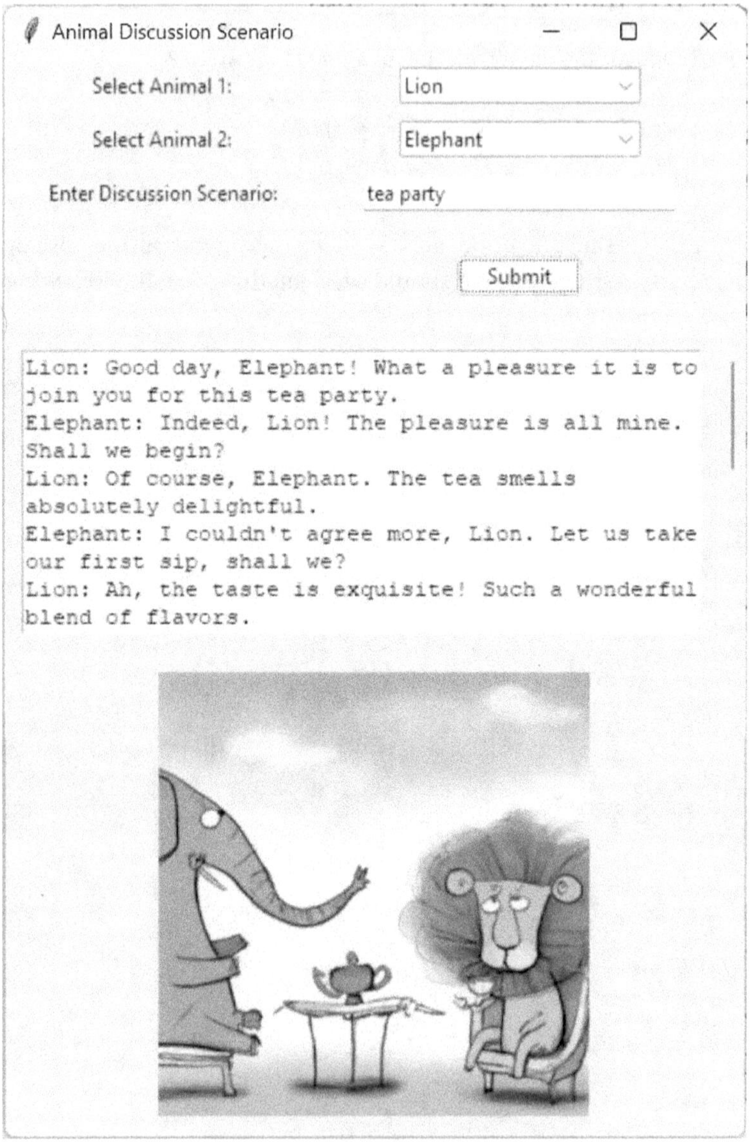

Figure 11. Story and Image

Creating a PDF from our Story

Although we can see our entire story in the UI, it would be nice to put the story in a form that we can share with others. Let's add a new function that leverages a Python module called **reportlab** that will let us do just that. First install report lab using pip:

```
1   pip install reportlab
```

Now, import the reportlab libraries we need for creating the pdf:

```
1   from reportlab.lib.pagesizes import letter
2   from reportlab.lib.units import inch
3   from reportlab.platypus import SimpleDocTemplate,
4   Image as ReportLabImage, Paragraph
5   from reportlab.lib.styles import
6                           getSampleStyleSheet
```

Now lets add a button to our UI to allow us to create the pdf file:

```
1   # Button to submit the details
2   create_pdf_btn = ttk.Button(
3       app, text="Create Pdf", command=
4           lambda: create_pdf(
5               result_text.get(1.0, tk.END)))
6   create_pdf_btn.grid(column=2, row=3,
7                       padx=10, pady=20)
```

Because we are passing the resulting text as a parameter in the button command, we needed to use a Python lambda expression to allow us to wrap the create_pdf call.

Next, we want to ensure that we can generate the story image. In order to make it easy, and instead of trying to extract the image from the Tk control, we'll just save the image file in as soon as we generate it with the display_image_from_url function:

```
1   def display_image_from_url(image_holder, url):
2       # Fetch the image from the URL
3       response = requests.get(url)
4       image_data = BytesIO(response.content)
5
6       # Open and display the image
7       # using PIL and tkinter
8       image = Image.open(image_data)
9
10      # Save the image as a PNG to use
11      # for pdf export
12      image.save(pil_image_path, "PNG")
13
14      photo = ImageTk.PhotoImage(image)
15
16      update_label_with_new_image(image_holder,
17                                          photo)
18      return image
```

Now we have everything we need to create the pdf so let's write our create_pdf function to handle the file generation.

The function create_pdf is designed to generate a PDF document from a given dialog text. First, it checks if the provided dialog_text is empty, and if so, it displays an error message urging the user to generate the dialog before proceeding. If the dialog text is available, it initializes the PDF document using the SimpleDocTemplate function with the filename "**output.pdf**" and sets the page size to the standard letter size. The function then establishes a contents list to compile the items that will go into the PDF. Our saved png image (from our previous display_image_from_url call) is resized to specific dimensions and is appended to the list. The provided dialog text is then formatted to ensure line breaks are appropriately translated for the PDF format. This formatted text is turned into a styled paragraph which is then added to the PDF contents. Finally, the PDF document is built with the specified contents. Upon successful creation of the PDF, a message box is displayed to notify the user that the PDF has been successfully generated.

```
1   pil_image_path = "c:\\temp\\temp__storytelling_image.png"
2
3   # This function will create the PDF
4   def create_pdf(dialog_text):
5       if  len(dialog_text) == 0:
6           messagebox.showerror("Error",
7               "Please generate the dialog first!")
8           return
9
10      # 3. Create a PDF with both the extracted
11      #    image and some text
12      doc = SimpleDocTemplate("output.pdf", pagesize=letter)
13
14      # Create the contents list for the PDF
15      contents = []
16
17      # Add the extracted image
18      # Adjust width and height as needed
19      img = ReportLabImage(pil_image_path,
20          width=2.5*inch,
21          height=2.5*inch)
22      contents.append(img)
23
24      # Add some text
25      dialog_text = '<br/>' + dialog_text
26      dialog_text = dialog_text.replace('\n',
27                          '<br/><br/>')
28      styles = getSampleStyleSheet()
29      paragraph = Paragraph(dialog_text,
30                          styles['Normal'])
31      contents.append(paragraph)
32
33      # Build the PDF
```

```
34    doc.build(contents)
35
36    # message box saying we
37    # finished generating the PDF
38    messagebox.showinfo("PDF Created", "PDF
39       created successfully!")
```

Generating the PDF

First let's choose a more confrontational story by pitting the lion against the elephant in a duel. Clicking the submit button yields the following result.

Figure 12. Lion vs Elephant

Now click the **create pdf** button and it should quickly generate a PDF called output PDF. Here are the results showing in Adobe Acrobat:

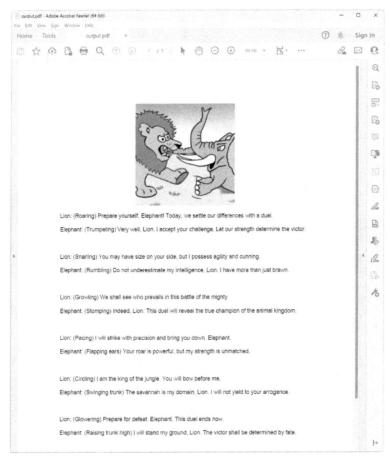

Figure 13. Generated PDF

Securing API Keys with `python-dotenv`

Exposing API keys and sensitive data in our code is a serious security risk. Thankfully, `python-dotenv` provides a way to separate our API key configuration from our code, which also simplifies configuration in different environments. Here's a detailed explanation on how we can use `python-dotenv` to keep our API keys secure.

What is `python-dotenv`?

`python-dotenv` is a Python library that allows us to specify environment variables in a `.env` file. This keeps sensitive data, like API keys, separate from the source code. Once specified, these variables can be read into our Python environment at runtime.

Steps to Secure Your API Key:

Assigning our API key directly in our Python code is dangerous; here are the top 3 reasons.

1. **Version Control Exposure**: If you commit your code with the API key to version control systems like Git, your key becomes part of the repository's history. Anyone with access to the repository can see and misuse your key, especially if the repository is public.
2. **Accidental Sharing**: There's a risk of unintentionally revealing your API key when sharing your code, whether with colleagues, on forums, or other platforms. An accidental leak can lead to unauthorized access.
3. **Financial Implications**: For services that charge based on usage, unauthorized access using your leaked API key can result in unexpected and potentially high charges.

To circumvent these security challenges, we'll integrate a library named **dotenv** into our code. This tool allows us to store our API key in a safer and more discreet location than our codebase.

4. **Installation**: First, you need to install the `python-dotenv` library. Use pip for this:

```
1    pip install python-dotenv
```

5. **Setting Up .env File**: Create a .env file in the root directory of your project. Inside this file, you can set your API key:

```
1    OPENAI_API_KEY=YourActualAPIKeyHere
```

6. **Accessing the API Key in Your Python Code**: With the .env file in place, you can now modify your Python code to read from this file:

```
1    import os
2    from dotenv import load_dotenv
3
4    # Load the .env file
5    load_dotenv()
6
7    # Access the API key
8    openai_api_key = os.getenv('OPENAI_API_KEY')
```

Where does python-dotenv look for the .env file?

- By default, python-dotenv will look for a .env file in the same directory as the one where load_dotenv is called. If your project structure is more complex and the .env file is not in the root directory, you can provide a path to the .env file as an argument to load_dotenv().
- If you don't want to use a .env file, you can also set environment variables directly in your environment or use other mechanisms your platform provides for this. If a variable with the same name as one in your .env file exists in your actual environment, the real environment variable will take precedence over the .env file. This is handy when you want to change the environment variable for different stages of your application (e.g., development, testing, production).

Important Notes:

- **Gitignore**: Ensure you add the `.env` file to your `.gitignore` to prevent it from being committed to version control systems like Git. This is crucial to keeping your secrets, well, secret.
- **Environment-Specific Files**: For different environments (development, production, staging, etc.), you can have different `.env` files, like `.env.dev`, `.env.prod`, and so on. This helps in keeping environment-specific configurations separate.
- **No Default Values**: If `os.getenv` doesn't find the specified environment variable, it will return `None`. If you expect a default value when the key is not present, you can provide it as the second argument, like: `os.getenv('KEY_NAME', 'default_value')`. **Note**: Your default_value should probably **not** be your actual key, though, if you plan on sharing the code or putting it into a public source control repository.

By following the above steps and guidelines, you can ensure that your API keys and sensitive data remain secure and separated from your application's codebase.

Conclusion

Throughout this chapter, we dived deep into the synergistic blend of OpenAI's capabilities with Python's versatile Tk and `Tkinter` libraries. We meticulously crafted an application that not only showcased the power of machine learning but also placed the user in the driver's seat, enabling them to bring to life unique stories involving two animals of their choice in a defined scenario. The seamless integration of these libraries offers a testament to the boundless potential when user-friendly interfaces meet AI-driven content generation. As this chapter comes to an end, even more possibilities lie ahead. We're about to unveil the secrets of using ChatGPT to craft a universal translator, turning spoken words from one language seamlessly into another. Turn the page and witness the future of communication!

Creating your own Babel Fish

Figure 14. Babel Fish

Introduction

Imagine a universe teeming with diverse and vibrant alien civilizations, each speaking their own enigmatic, tongue-twisting language. In Douglas Adams' whimsically brilliant *Hitchhiker's Guide to the Galaxy*, the secret to comprehending these extraterrestrial languages wasn't a fancy gadget or a superhuman ability. It was a fish! Not just any fish, but the Babel Fish, a miraculous creature that, when tucked into one's ear, decoded any and all alien speech, rendering it instantly understandable to the listener. Now, leapfrog from that interstellar realm to our own digital age, and we're on the cusp of an equally wondrous invention: the ChatGPT Python app. No wet, squishy fish required — just a state-of-the-art algorithm that captures your spoken word and translates it, with mind-blowing accuracy, into any language you desire. From the vistas of the Milky Way to the audio of your headset, the dream of universal communication is about to become a reality.

Library Setup

To begin our journey creating a translation marvel, we'll build a foundation with essential Python libraries. These will empower our application to:

- Listen to spoken words and capture them as a WAV file.
- Transcribe the recorded speech leveraging the prowess of ChatGPT's Whisper model.
- Seamlessly translate the transcription using the advanced chatgpt3-turbo model.
- Finally, breathe life into our translated text by vocalizing it through Google's Text-to-Speech service.

With these tools at our disposal, we're poised to bridge languages and connect voices from across the globe!

Let's install the necessary Python libraries for our project

```
1  pip install python-dotenv sounddevice numpy pydub
2             pygame gtts wavio
```

And here is an explanation of each of them:

1. **dotenv**: This library is used to read key-value pairs from a .env file and add them to the environment variables. It's especially useful for managing secret keys, database credentials, or other configuration variables without hardcoding them into the application. We use it here to read our OPEN AI Key from the .env file to make the key a little more secure.

2. **sounddevice**: This Python module provides bindings to the PortAudio library and enables you to work with audio data. It can be used to play and record audio using a variety of backend drivers. We use it in our babel fish app in order to record speech from the microphone.

3. **wavio**: A Python module that defines functions to read and write WAV files using numpy arrays. It's a convenient tool when you want to handle WAV file input/output in conjunction with numpy operations. We'll be using wavio to capture audio data from the sounddevice recording into a WAV file.

4. **pygame**: A cross-platform set of Python modules designed for writing video games. It provides functionalities like creating windows, drawing shapes, capturing mouse events, and playing sounds. Though designed for games, pygame can be used for other multimedia tasks as well. In our case we are stealing pygame's awesome ability to play speech from the speaker of the computer.

5. **gtts (Google Text-to-Speech)**: A Python library and CLI tool that interfaces with Google Translate's text-to-speech API. You can write spoken mp3 data to a file, a file-like object, or stdout. This means you can very easily use this library to convert a text string into spoken words.

Creating the Babel Fish Shell

To begin, we'll craft a user interface (UI) that allows users to specify their desired source and target languages for translation. If you recall from Chapter 2, we utilized the **Tk** library for our UI needs. We'll be employing this trusty library once more for our Babel Fish shell.

Here's a breakdown of the UI elements we're going to implement:

- **Language Dropdowns**: Two dropdown menus where users can select the 'input' and 'output' languages for translation.
- **Duration Dropdown**: This will allow users to determine the length of the recording.
- **Record Button**: A prominent button enabling users to initiate the recording of the speech they wish to translate.
- **Status Label**: This essential feature will keep users informed about the app's ongoing processes, ensuring they're always in the loop.

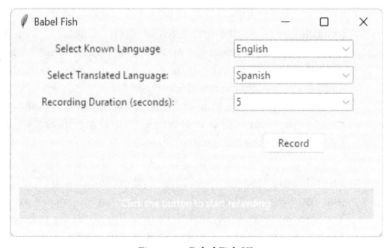

Figure 15. Babel Fish UI

Let's take a look at what that code looks like for the UI

```python
# create a dictionary to store the languages and
# their corresponding codes
languages = {'English': 'en', 'Spanish': 'es',
             'French': 'fr', 'German': 'de',
             'Russian': 'ru', 'Chinese': 'zh'}


app = tk.Tk()
app.title("Babel Fish")
style = ttk.Style()

# Label and ComboBox for the first animal
label1 = ttk.Label(app, text="Select Known Language")
label1.grid(column=0, row=0, padx=10, pady=5)
combo1 = ttk.Combobox(
    app, values=list(languages.keys()))
combo1.grid(column=1, row=0, padx=10, pady=5)
combo1.set("English")

# Label and ComboBox for the second animal
label2 = ttk.Label(app,
    text="Select Translated Language:")
label2.grid(column=0, row=1, padx=10, pady=5)
combo2 = ttk.Combobox(
    app, values=list(languages.keys()))
combo2.grid(column=1, row=1, padx=10, pady=5)
combo2.set("Spanish")

label_recording_duration = tk.Label(app,
        text="Recording Duration (seconds):")
label_recording_duration.grid(column=0, row=2,
  padx=10, pady=5)
combo_duration = ttk.Combobox(app, values=[5, 10, 15,
    20, 25, 30])
combo_duration.grid(column=1, row=2, padx=10, pady=5)
```

```
36   combo_duration.set(5)
37
38   # Button to submit the text to translate
39   submit_btn = ttk.Button(app, text="Record",
40       command=submit)
41   submit_btn.grid(column=1, row=3, padx=10, pady=20)
42   label_recording = tk.Label(app,
43               text="Click the button to start recording",
44               bg="lightgray", fg="white", width=60,
45               height=2)
46   label_recording.grid(column=0, columnspan=2, row=8,
47                        padx=10, pady=20)
48
49   app.mainloop()
```

The code initializes a graphical user interface (GUI) application using the Tkinter library, specifically named "**Babel Fish**".

There are two dropdown menus (ComboBox) to select languages. The first dropdown allows users to pick the language they're speaking or inputting. It's labeled "Select Known Language" and provides options such as English, Spanish, French, German, and Russian. By default, it's set to "English".

The second dropdown is labeled "Select Translated Language" and lets users choose the desired output language for the translation. It offers the same set of language choices and defaults to "Spanish".

Following the language selectors, there's another dropdown menu for users to specify the recording duration in seconds. It offers preset values ranging from 5 to 30 seconds, with a default setting of 5 seconds.

There's a button labeled "Record" that, when clicked, triggers a function called submit that will call the submit method to do the whole recording and translation.

Below this button, a label provides users with instructions, indicating they should click the button to start recording. This label has a light gray background and white text.

Finally, the GUI event loop is started with app.mainloop(), ensuring the application remains open and responsive to user interactions.

Submit (Record) Function

When you hit that Record button, magic happens! It activates the submit function which initiates a sequence of tasks from capturing your voice, transcribing what you said, translating it flawlessly, and then providing audio of the result. 🎤 Let's uncover the wonders behind these processes!

Analyzing the submit Method

Drilling down into the submit method, we've distilled the process into a sequence of straightforward steps:

1. **capture_audio**: This function acquires the user's spoken words.
2. **transcribe**: Converts the captured audio into textual format.
3. **translate**: Processes the transcribed text and converts it into the user-selected language.
4. **text_to_speech**: Gives voice to the translated text, enabling the user to hear the translation.

Here's a closer look at the submit method's implementation:

```
1   def submit():
2
3       set_wait_cursor()
4
5       # 1. Capture Audio
6       capture_audio()
7
8       # 2. Transcribe the Audio
9       transcription = transcribe()
10
11      # 3. Translate the Transcribed Audio
12      resulting_translation = translate(
13          combo1.get(), combo2.get(), transcription)
14
15      # 4. Voice the Translated Text
16      text_to_speech(resulting_translation, combo2.get())
17
18      reset_status()
19      set_normal_cursor()
```

This method is organized in such a way as to ensure a seamless transition from capturing the user's speech to presenting the audible translation.

Recording Speech

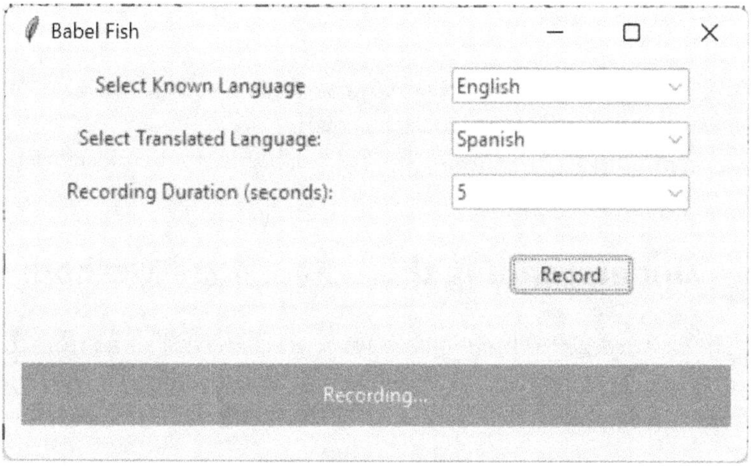

Figure 16. Recording State

When the user clicks the Record button, the status Label will turn red and start recording speech for the duration chosen in the dropdown. Let's dig deeper into the capture_audio method shown below:

```
1   def capture_audio():
2       # Indicate start of recording
3       label_recording.config(text="Recording...", bg="red")
4       app.update()
5
6       # get number of seconds from dropdown
7       duration = int(combo_duration.get())
8       samplerate = 44100
9       audio = sd.rec(int(samplerate * duration),
10                  samplerate=samplerate, channels=2,
11                  dtype='int16')
12      sd.wait()
13
```

```
14      label_recording.config(text="Finished Recording",
15         bg="green")
16
17      app.update()
18
19      # Save the numpy array to a WAV file using wavio
20      wav_path = "c:\\temp\\myrecording.wav"
21      wavio.write(wav_path, audio, samplerate, sampwidth=2)
```

Understanding the `capture_audio` Method

The `capture_audio` function's main goal is to record audio from the user for a specified duration and then save that audio to a WAV file. Here's a step-by-step explanation of the method:

1. **Letting user know we are recording**:

```
1          label_recording.config(text="Recording...", bg="red")
2          app.update()
```

   - The `label_recording` is updated to display the text "Recording...", and its background color is set to red. This provides visual feedback to the user that recording is in progress.
   - `app.update()` is then called to refresh the GUI, ensuring that the updated label is immediately visible.

2. **Setting Up the Recording**:

```
1      # get duration in seconds from the dropdown
2      duration = int(combo_duration.get())
3      samplerate = 44100
```

   - The function retrieves the desired recording duration from the `combo_duration` dropdown and converts it to an integer, storing it in the `duration` variable.

- The samplerate is set to 44,100 Hz (or 44.1 kHz), which is a common sample rate used in audio recording, especially for music and vocalization.

3. **Recording the Audio**:

```
1    audio = sd.rec(int(samplerate * duration),
2                   samplerate=samplerate, channels=2,
3                   dtype='int16')
4    sd.wait()
```

- The function invokes sd.rec() from the sounddevice library to start recording audio. Several parameters are passed:
- The total number of samples to record, computed as the product of samplerate and duration.
- The samplerate itself.
- The number of channels (2, for stereo recording).
- The data type for the audio data (int16 which represents 16-bit PCM coding).
- Following this, sd.wait() is called to ensure the program waits until the recording is completed.

4. **Finishing the Recording**:

```
1    label_recording.config(text="Finished Recording",
2                                bg="green")
3    app.update()
```

- Once the recording is done, the label_recording is updated again to display "Finished Recording" with a green background. This tells the user that the recording process has successfully completed.
- Another app.update() ensures that these GUI changes are displayed promptly.

5. **Saving the Audio Data**:

```
1    # Save the numpy array to a WAV file using wavio
2    wav_path = "c:\\temp\\myrecording.wav"
3    wavio.write(wav_path, audio, samplerate, sampwidth=2)
```

- The recorded audio data, which is stored in the audio numpy array, is saved to a WAV file. The wavio.write() function is used for this purpose. This function takes several arguments:

    - The file path where the WAV file should be saved. ("c:\\temp\\myrecording.wav" in this case).
    - The audio data itself (audio).
    - The sample rate (samplerate).
    - The sample width (sampwidth=2 indicates 16-bit samples since 2 bytes equal 16 bits).

In Summary

The capture_audio function seamlessly handles the process of capturing the user's speech, updating the GUI to indicate progress, and saving the audio data as a WAV file.

Transcribing Speech

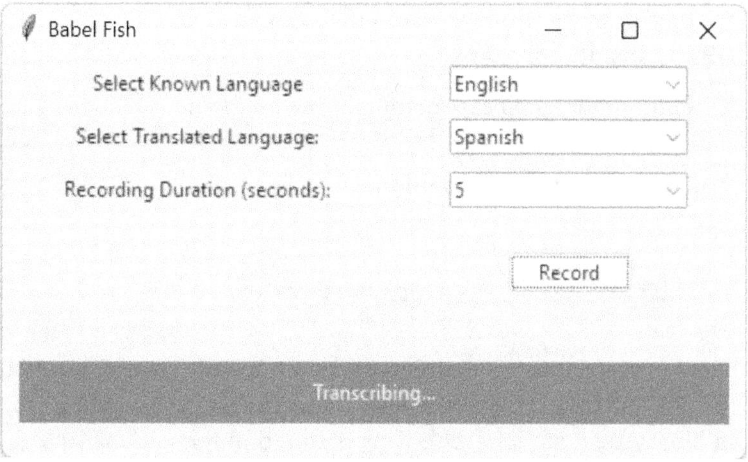

Figure 17. Transcribing the Speech

Here is where we take full advantages of the wisdom of ChatGPT. ChatGPT not only has the ability to respond to text, ChatGPT is trained on audio as well. It is capable of taking our WAV file and transcribing it into text. ChatGPT works on other formats as well, but for the purpose of this exercise, we used the WAV file. Below is the code that calls ChatGPT's transcribe method to get the representational text. Note it's a fairly short method!

```
1   def transcribe():
2       audio_file = open("c:\\temp\\myrecording.wav", "rb")
3       set_label("Transcribing...")
4       transcription = openai.Audio.transcribe(
5           model='whisper-1',
6           file=audio_file)
7       audio_file.close()
8       print('transcription: ' +
9               f'{transcription["text"]}\n\n')
10      return transcription["text"]
```

Understanding the `transcribe` Method

The `transcribe` function encapsulates the process of converting spoken language (from an audio file) into written text using Chat-GPT's capabilities.

Here's a step-by-step explanation of the method:

1. **Opening the Audio File:**

```
1   audio_file = open("c:\\temp\\myrecording.wav", "rb")
```

The function starts by opening the audio file we created from our previous method `capture_audio` (`"c:\\temp\\myrecording.wav"`) in binary read mode (`"rb"`). This is stored in the variable `audio_-file`.

2. **Updating User Feedback:**

```
1   set_label("Transcribing...")
```

The `set_label` function is invoked with the argument "Transcribing...". It serves to inform the user in the status label that the transcribing process is underway.

3. **Transcription using ChatGPT:**

```
1   transcription = openai.Audio.transcribe(
2           model='whisper-1', file=audio_file)
```

ChatGPT's transcription capabilities are harnessed via the `openai.Audio.transcribe` method. Two arguments are provided:

- `model='whisper-1'`: This specifies the model to use for the transcription. 'whisper-1' is a model designed for audio transcription.
- `file=audio_file`: This is the audio file we want to transcribe (generated in capture_audio).
- The resulting transcription is stored in the `transcription` variable.

4. **Cleaning Up**:

```
audio_file.close()
```

The audio file (`audio_file`) is closed using the `close` method. This ensures that system resources are freed up after they are no longer needed.

5. **Printing and Returning**:

```
print('transcription: ' + f'{transcription["text"]}
                        \n\n')
return transcription["text"]
```

The transcribed text is printed to the console for debugging purposes and finally, the `transcription` is returned from the function. This allows other parts of the program to access and make use of the transcribed text.

Note: we need to extract the text from the response using the `text` key in order to a retrieve the string of the transcribed text returned by the `Audio.transcribe` method.

In Summary

The `transcribe` function provides a streamlined process of turning speech (captured in a WAV file) into textual content using ChatGPT's 'whisper-1' model. This showcases the versatility of ChatGPT, demonstrating its usefulness not only in text-based interactions but also in handling audio data.

Translating Speech

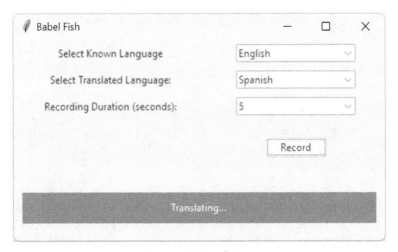

Figure 18. Translation

By feeding the API with a well-structured prompt, users can effortlessly instruct ChatGPT to translate text from one language to another. This doesn't only involve a simple word-for-word translation, but it also considers the context, idioms, and cultural nuances of the source and target languages.

Understanding the `translate` Method

The translate method takes our native text and translates it into a corresponding language text. The default for our application is **English** to **Spanish**, but you can choose any language you want from the dropdown. ChatGPT actually handles the translation of quite a few more languages. Here are some of them:

- English
- Spanish
- French
- German
- Chinese (Simplified)
- Chinese (Traditional)
- Russian
- Italian
- Portuguese
- Dutch
- Japanese
- Korean
- Arabic
- Swedish
- Danish
- Finnish
- Norwegian
- Turkish
- Polish
- Greek
- Hebrew
- Hindi
- Indonesian
- Thai
- Hungarian
- Czech

- Romanian
- Bulgarian
- Croatian
- Ukrainian
- Slovak
- Lithuanian
- Slovenian
- Estonian
- Latvian
- Bengali
- Punjabi
- Gujarati
- Marathi
- Telugu
- Malayalam
- Kannada
- Oriya
- Malay
- Filipino
- Vietnamese

Note: While ChatGPT can translate between these languages, the quality and fluency of translations might vary. For professional or critical translations, specialized translation services or software are recommended.

```
1  def translate(language1, language2, text):
2      set_label("Translating...")
3      prompt = f"Translate the following from
4                  {language1} to {language2}: {text}"
5      messages = [{'role': 'user', 'content': prompt}]
6      response = openai.ChatCompletion.create(
7          model="gpt-3.5-turbo",
8          messages=messages,
9          temperature=0.8,
10         top_p=1.0,
11         frequency_penalty=0.0,
12         presence_penalty=0.6,
13     )
14
15     chat_gpt_translation =
16       response["choices"][0]["message"]["content"]
17     print('translation: ' + chat_gpt_translation)
18     return chat_gpt_translation
```

Method Breakdown

Setting the Label

```
1   set_label("Translating...")
```

The set_label function updates the status to "Translating...", providing feedback to the user that the system is in the process of translating the text.

Prompt Construction

```
1  prompt = f"Translate the following from {language1} to
2              {language2}: {text}"
```

This step constructs a string named prompt. It serves as an instruction for the GPT-3.5-turbo model to execute the translation task. For instance, when translating the word "Hello" from English to Spanish, the constructed prompt reads: "Translate the following from English to Spanish: Hello".

Creating the Messages Array

```
1   messages = [{'role': 'user', 'content': prompt}]
```

Here, the message is structured in a format that the GPT-3.5-turbo chat model anticipates. Though the model is designed to handle a sequence of conversational messages, in our scenario, the messages array houses a single entry, serving as the translation prompt.

Executing the API Call

```
1   response = openai.ChatCompletion.create(
2       model="gpt-3.5-turbo",
3       messages=messages,
4       temperature=0.8,
5       top_p=1.0,
6       frequency_penalty=0.0,
7       presence_penalty=0.6,
8   )
```

In this phase, a request is dispatched to the OpenAI's API with the following key parameters:

- **model**: Refers to the specific iteration of the model in use, which in our case is "gpt-3.5-turbo".
- **messages**: Encompasses the message array we sculpted in the prior step.
- **temperature**: Modulates the randomness in the model's replies. A figure nearing 0 produces more predictable outputs, while a value approaching 1 introduces greater randomness.

- **top_p**: Implements a cap for nucleus sampling, ascertaining that the accumulated probability for token selection remains below the specified threshold.
- **frequency_penalty** & **presence_penalty**: These parameters tune the model's propensity to select tokens based on their recurrent appearance in the dataset.

Following the API call, a `response` is received. Nested within this response structure is our desired translation.

Extracting the Response

```
1    chat_gpt_translation =
2        response["choices"][0]["message"]["content"]
```

Lastly, the method extracts and returns the translated content from the deep-seated layers of the response.

In Summary

The bulk of this method is calling the openapi `ChatCompletion` method with a prompt instructing ChatGPT to translate from one language to another. We retrieve the contents of the response from this call and return the translated text.

Vocalizing the Text

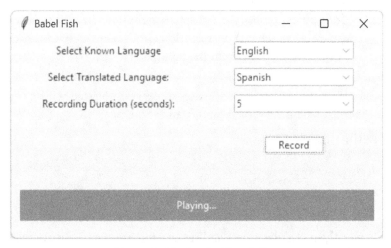

Figure 19. Playing the Translation

This transition from text to speech isn't just about audibly representing words, but also about capturing the right tone, pace, and emphasis, making the listening experience as natural and engaging as possible. Through this process, we will be employing specific Python libraries to make our translated text not just readable, but also listenable. Whether for accessibility reasons, multitasking, or simply a preference for audio content, vocalizing text enriches the user experience, adding a dynamic dimension to our application.

Exploring the `text_to_speech` Method

With our translated text in hand, it's time to give it a voice! We'll tap into Google's robust text-to-speech engine to convert our translations into crisp MP3 audio files. And thanks to pygame, we'll seamlessly broadcast it right through your computer's speakers.

Let's look at the code:

```
1    def text_to_speech(translated_text, language):
2
3        set_label("Playing...")
4        # Convert Translated Text to Speech using Google's
5        # text-to-speech library
6        tts = gTTS(translated_text, lang=languages[language],
7                   slow=False)
8
9        # save the results in a temporary mp3 file
10       tts.save('C:\\temp\\hello.mp3')
11
12       # Initialize pygame mixer
13       pygame.mixer.init()
14       pygame.mixer.music.load('C:\\temp\\hello.mp3')
15       pygame.mixer.music.play()
16
17
18   # If you want to keep the program running until
19   # the audio is done playing:
20       while pygame.mixer.music.get_busy():
21           pygame.time.Clock().tick(10)   # This will wait
22                                          # and let the music
23                                          # play.
24
25       # close the mp3 file
26       pygame.mixer.music.stop()
27       pygame.mixer.quit()
28       os.remove('C:\\temp\\hello.mp3')
```

The text_to_speech **Function Explained**

The text_to_speech function is an elegant blend of text conversion and audio playback capabilities. Here's a step-by-step breakdown:

1. **Setting Application Status**:

```
1    set_label("Playing...")
```

The status on our application is updated to "Playing..." to provide feedback to the user that the audio playback is in progress.

2. **Text Conversion to Speech:**

```
1    tts = gTTS(translated_text, lang=languages[language], slo\
2    w=False)
```

Using Google's text-to-speech (gTTS) library, the translated text is converted into speech. The language for the speech is determined by the language variable, which fetches the respective language code from the languages dictionary.

3. **Save as MP3:**

```
1    tts.save('C:\\temp\\hello.mp3')
```

The audio obtained from the conversion is then saved temporarily as an MP3 file named 'hello.mp3' in the specified directory.

4. **Initialize and Play with pygame:**

```
1    pygame.mixer.init()
2    pygame.mixer.music.load('C:\\temp\\hello.mp3')
3    pygame.mixer.music.play()
```

To play our saved audio file, we make use of the pygame library. First, the mixer is initialized, then our saved MP3 file is loaded, and finally, it's played.

5. **Hold the Execution Until Audio Completion:**

```
1    while pygame.mixer.music.get_busy():
2        pygame.time.Clock().tick(10)
```

To ensure the function doesn't move on before the audio completes, the code waits for the audio to finish playing. The `tick` function allows the system to periodically check if the audio is still playing.

6. **Cleanup:**

```
1    pygame.mixer.music.stop()
2    pygame.mixer.quit()
3    os.remove('C:\\temp\\hello.mp3')
```

Once the audio has been played, these cleanup steps are executed. The audio playback is stopped, the mixer exits out, and the temporary MP3 file is deleted to free up space.

In Summary

This function effortlessly transforms translated text into crystal-clear audio,all with a dash of code magic. By harnessing the power of Google's text-to-speech for translation and pygame for audio playback, we've brought our vision of an advanced AI translator to life!

Concluding the Babel Fish Journey

Throughout our exploration, we've journeyed from the humble beginnings of capturing raw audio to the exhilarating finale of audibly communicating translated messages. Our BabelFish Python app stands as a practical example of illustrating the harmonious blend of various technologies: capturing live speech, transcribing it using ChatGPT's Whisper model, translating across languages with

ChatGPT's turbo engine, and finally, echoing back to us through Google's text-to-speech rendered by pygame.

The horizon for this tool is vast. Imagine integrating real-time translation for video conferences or business meetings, ensuring that everyone, regardless of their native tongue, stays on the same page. Or perhaps, with a bit of tweaking, our app could aid in learning and practicing new languages, acting as a tutor that corrects pronunciation and grammar. The foundations laid here can also be repurposed for voice-activated home automation, or even interactive voice response systems for businesses. The potential is limited only by our imagination. As we close this chapter, it's thrilling to envision where this BabelFish app could lead us next, unlocking doors to a multilingual world!

Three Ingredient Recipe Creater

Figure 20. Robot Making a Recipe

Get Ready for an Epic Culinary Adventure!

Last night, I swung open my fridge door, and encountered a ghost town. There were just three survivors from the last grocery trip: an eggplant, a wedge of parmesan, and a lone roll. Now, any average Joe could toss them into a pan and hope for the best. But what if you could wave a wand and make a tantalizing recipe appear, tailored specifically for these three ingredients? Wish granted. In this chapter we produce unlikely feasts, supercharged by the remarkable Chat GPT API! Are you ready to become an overnight culinary wizard? Let's cook up some code magic!

Kickstarting Our Culinary Code Journey

Before diving into our recipe-generating code, let's ensure a pristine Python environment. This prevents potential conflicts with existing packages or dependencies. A virtual environment is our trusty kitchen where we'll be cooking this app, allowing us to know the exact libraries we're adding. Kick things off by setting up the virtual environment; if you're on a PC, execute the following command in your recipe project directory:

```
1    python -m venv recipe
```

Activating the Virtual Kitchen

To bring our virtual environment to life on a PC, we'll use the handy activate script that our virtual environment so thoughtfully provided. From the directory where you whipped up your virtual environment, execute the following (for our PC chefs):

```
1    .\recipe\Scripts\activate.bat
```

For our Linux culinary coders, stir things up with:

```
1  source recipe/bin/activate
```

Prepping the Kitchen

Let the coding feast begin! With our kitchen prepped, it's time to stock it with the essential tools. Install the required packages for our Flask application:

```
1  pip install flask openai render_template python-dotenv
```

The Home Page

Now let's cook! Begin by writing a template for our home page, index.html. Note that this template goes in a folder of our app called templates in order for the template rendering engine (jinja2) to find it.

```
1   <!DOCTYPE html>
2   <html>
3   <head>
4       <title>Recipe Generator</title>
5   </head>
6   <body>
7       <h2>Input 3 Ingredients</h2>
8       <form action="/generate_recipe" method="post">
9           <input type="text" name="ingredient"
10            placeholder="Ingredient 1" required>
11          <input type="text" name="ingredient"
12            placeholder="Ingredient 2" required>
13          <input type="text" name="ingredient"
14            placeholder="Ingredient 3" required>
```

```
15              <input type="submit" value="Generate Recipe">
16         </form>
17    </body>
18    </html>
```

Let's break down the html and focus on the core elements of the form and its associated components:

```
1    <form action="/generate_recipe" method="post">
```

- **<form>**: This is the beginning of a form element. Everything inside it will be part of the user input collection mechanism.
- action="/generate_recipe" specifies the server URL to which the form data should be sent after submission. In this instance, the form data will be sent to the /generate_recipe route on the server.
- method="post" indicates the HTTP method used for sending the data. The POST method is chosen for sending data securely.

```
1    <input type="text" name="ingredient"
2      placeholder="Ingredient 1" required>
3    <input type="text" name="ingredient"
4     placeholder="Ingredient 2" required>
5    <input type="text" name="ingredient"
6     placeholder="Ingredient 3" required>
```

- **<input>**: These tags create text boxes where users can type in the ingredients.
- type="text" specifies that they are text input fields.
- name="ingredient" denotes the name of the data when collected from the form. All three inputs have the same name ingredient, so they will be retrieved as a list from the server.

- `placeholder="Ingredient X"` is a hint displayed in the text box before user input. It guides users on what to enter.
- `required` means the user has to fill this input before submitting the form.

```
1    <input type="submit" value="Generate Recipe">
```

- `<input>`: This creates a button for submitting the form.

  - `type="submit"` denotes that it's a submit button. When clicked, it will send the form data to the server.
  - `value="Generate Recipe"` is the text that appears on the button, guiding the user to click it after entering the ingredients.

```
1    </form>
```

- `</form>`: This closes the form tag. Everything between the opening `<form>` and this closing `</form>` tag is considered part of the form.

In essence, this portion of the HTML code sets up an input mechanism for users to submit three ingredients and then request a recipe based on those inputs. The data is sent securely using the POST method to the `/generate_recipe` endpoint on the server.

If we look at the template in the browser it will look something like the following:

Input 3 Ingredients

Figure 21. Raw Template in Browser

Rendering the Template in Flask

The bare bones needed to render our Jinja2 template is shown
below. We simply import flask and the render_template function
and use that to render the home page.

```
1  from flask import Flask, render_template
2
3  app = Flask(__name__)
4
5  @app.route('/')
6  def index():
7      return render_template('index.html')
```

Let's break down this code snippet step by step to understand its
workings in the context of Flask and template rendering:

1. **Imports**:

```
1      from flask import Flask, render_template
```

Here, we're importing the necessary components from the Flask
library: - Flask: This is the main class that we use to create our
Flask application instance. - render_template: This is a function
that Flask provides to render our Jinja2 templates.

2. **Flask App Instance**:

```
1      app = Flask(__name__)
```

Instantiate the Flask application using app = Flask(__name__).
This creates an instance of the Flask class which will be our web
application.

3. **Route Decorator**:

```
1    @app.route('/')
```

The @app.route('/') is a decorator provided by Flask. This decorator tells Flask that the following function (in this case index()) should be executed when the root URL ('/') of the application is accessed. In simpler terms, when someone visits the home page of our app, this function gets called.

4. View Function:

```
1    def index():
2        return render_template('index.html')
```

This function, named index, is what Flask refers to as a "view function." When this function is invoked by Flask (due to its association with the '/' route), it executes the code within it. In this function, we're using the render_template function to render the index.html template.

The render_template function looks inside the templates folder of your Flask application for the file named index.html. Once it finds this file, it processes any Jinja2 templating commands (if present) and then returns the resulting HTML.

The returned HTML is then sent to the client's browser by Flask, so the user will see the contents of index.html when they visit the root URL of the application.

In essence, this simple code snippet sets up a basic Flask application where visiting the home page will display the contents of the rendered HTML template named index.html.

Running the App

When you install Flask with pip into your virtual environment, it actually installs an executable application called flask.exe. You can use this command to run your web server on your Flask code with the following command:

```
flask --app recipe run
```

The application by default will run on localhost on port 5000. If you open any browser at that location you will see the home page of our application:

Figure 22. Running Flask App

Styling the Home Page

To apply styles to our homepage, create a static folder within our app directory and, within that, a subfolder named css.

Figure 23. Location of css

In this folder, we will place a new file called style.css. Now let's style our application:

```
1   /* Base Styling */
2   body {
3     font-family: Arial, sans-serif;
4     background-color: #f4f4f4;
5     margin: 0;
6     padding: 0;
7   }
8
9   /* Centered Form Styling */
10  form {
11    max-width: 300px;
12    margin: 50px auto;
13    padding: 20px;
14    background-color: #fff;
15    box-shadow: 0 0 20px rgba(0, 0, 0, 0.1);
16    border-radius: 8px;
17  }
18
19  h2 {
20    text-align: center;
21    margin-bottom: 20px;
22  }
23
24  /* Input Styling */
25  input[type="text"] {
26    width: 95%;
27    padding: 10px;
28    margin-bottom: 10px;
29    border: 1px solid #ccc;
30    border-radius: 4px;
31  }
32
33  /* Button Styling */
34  input[type="submit"] {
35    width: 100%;
```

```
36    background-color: #007bff;
37    color: #fff;
38    padding: 10px;
39    border: none;
40    border-radius: 4px;
41    cursor: pointer;
42    transition: background-color 0.3s ease;
43  }
44
45  input[type="submit"]:hover {
46    background-color: #0056b3;
47  }
```

In this design, we've opted for a simple grey backdrop for our application, paired with clear input fields and button aesthetics. To bring these styles to life in our form, we must link the style.css file in our index.html template. Conveniently, Jinja2 provides the url_for function, ensuring a seamless integration of our style resources.

```
1  <html>
2    <head>
3      <title>Recipe Generator</title>
4      <link
5        rel="stylesheet"
6        href="{{ url_for('static',
7          filename='css/style.css') }}"
8      />
9    </head>
```

Now when we run our application in the browser we get the following polished form:

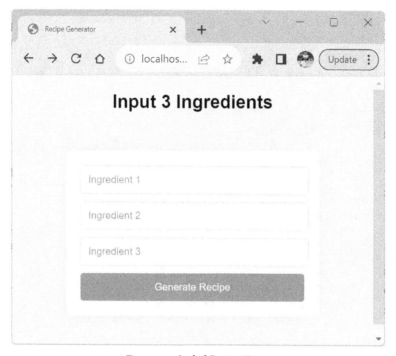

Figure 24. Styled Recipe Form

Harnessing ChatGPT within Flask for Culinary Creativity

With our template in place, it's time to tap into the magic of ChatGPT to generate recipes from the ingredients that our users provide. Our goal is to ensure that once the user enters their desired three ingredients and hits the 'Generate Recipe' button, we instantly connect to OpenAI's ChatGPT, requesting a delectable recipe in return.

Below is the full code that accomplishes this integration:

```
1    from flask import Flask, render_template, request
2    import openai
3    import os
4    from dotenv import load_dotenv
5
6    # Initialize environment variables
7    load_dotenv()
8
9    app = Flask(__name__)
10
11   # Securely fetch the API key using the dotenv library
12   openai.api_key = os.getenv('OPENAI_API_KEY')
13
14   @app.route('/')
15   def index():
16       # Display the main ingredient input page
17       return render_template('index.html')
18
19   @app.route('/generate_recipe', methods=['POST'])
20   def generate_recipe():
21       # Extract the three ingredients from the user's input
22       ingredients = request.form.getlist('ingredient')
23
24       if len(ingredients) != 3:
25           return "Kindly provide exactly 3 ingredients."
26
27       # Craft a conversational prompt for ChatGPT,
28       # specifying our needs
29       prompt = f"Craft a recipe in HTML using
30           {', '.join(ingredients)}.
31           Ensure the recipe ingredients appear at the top,
32           followed by the step-by-step instructions."
33
34       messages = [{'role': 'user', 'content': prompt}]
35
```

```
36      # Engage ChatGPT to receive the desired recipe
37      response = openai.ChatCompletion.create(
38          model="gpt-3.5-turbo",
39          messages=messages,
40          temperature=0.8,
41          top_p=1.0,
42          frequency_penalty=0.0,
43          presence_penalty=0.6,
44      )
45
46      # Extract the recipe from ChatGPT's response
47      recipe = response["choices"][0]["message"]["content"]
48
49      # Showcase the recipe on a new page
50      return render_template('recipe.html', recipe=recipe)
51
52  if __name__ == '__main__':
53      app.run(debug=True)
```

generate_recipe function explained

Initially, we set up a new Flask app and load the ChatGPT API key into it. The index function renders the home page (index.html) which prompts users for three ingredients.

Upon pressing the "generate" button, the generate_recipe function springs into action. It fetches the three ingredients from the form and places a call to the ChatGPT API for a tailored recipe. While this API interaction might seem reminiscent of our original storytelling API call, the core differentiation lies in the content of the prompt. Essentially, the magic behind these applications is the their ability to craft the perfect prompt!

Within this prompt, we direct the ChatGPT API to craft a comprehensive recipe, employing the trio of ingredients provided. Once the model processes the request, it dispenses a unique recipe, which we delegate to our second template, recipe.html.

```
1   <!DOCTYPE html>
2   <html>
3     <head>
4       <title>Generated Recipe</title>
5     </head>
6     <body>
7       <h2>Your Recipe:</h2>
8       <p>{{ recipe|safe }}</p>
9       <a href="/">Generate another recipe</a>
10    </body>
11  </html>
```

The entirety of our **recipe** is encapsulated within the HTML paragraph tag <p>. Utilizing the safe keyword permits us to embed HTML directly into the rendered template. Without this keyword, the HTML would be displayed with its tags visible rather than being seamlessly rendered.

Let's create a sandwich! If we input three ingredients to create a favorite Italian lunch, it looks like the following:

Figure 25. Entering Ingredients

Now when we hit the generate button, the app will spin for a while and eventually produce the following page in the rendered recipe.html page.

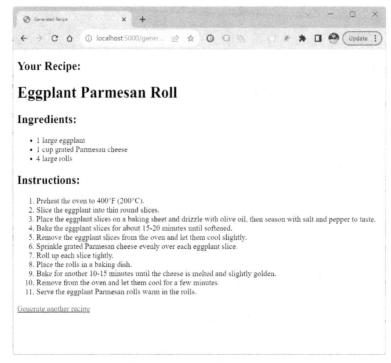

Figure 26. Recipe Generated

Choosing a Cuisine

Imagine embarking on a culinary journey using your three ingredients and also customizing the cuisine! Our recipe app is about to unveil a new world of flavors by letting you decide the destination of your next epicurean adventure. These dishes whisk you away to other countries, choosing favorite dishes that will make your taste buds tingle. Let's see how ChatGPT performs in the kitchen!

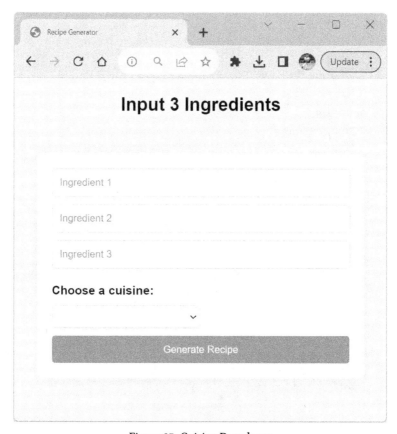

Figure 27. Cuisine Dropdown

We can pull more functionality out of recipe app by allowing the user to select their preferred cuisine when preparing their dish. Each cuisine suggests multiple popular international favorites. Let's see how we implement this in code:

Populating the Cuisine Dropdown

First of all, we'll add a list of cuisines to our Python recipe.py code

```
1  cuisines = [
2      "",
3      "Italian",
4      "Mexican",
5      "Chinese",
6      "Indian",
7      "Japanese",
8      "Thai",
9      "French",
10     "Mediterranean",
11     "American",
12     "Greek",
13  ]
```

In our index method, we'll pass these cuisines to the index.html template to be rendered in a dropdown on our home page.

```
1  @app.route('/')
2  def index():
3      # Display the main ingredient input page
4      return render_template('index.html',
5                          cuisines=cuisines)
```

Inside our template, **index.html**, we'll add the Jinja2 code to be able to render the cuisines as **options** in an html **select** tag. Jinja2 allows us to loop through each cuisine passed into the template and create a new option tag representing that cuisine.

```
1    <label class="subheading" for="cuisine">
2        Choose a cuisine:</label>
3    <select name="cuisine" id="cuisine">
4      {% for cuisine in cuisines %}
5      <option value="{{ cuisine|lower|replace(' ',
6                        '_') }}">
7        {{ cuisine }}
8      </option>
9      {% endfor %}
10   </select>
```

Styling the Cuisine Dropdown

We also want to style the dropdown so it is laid out properly. Here is the additional css needed:

```
1    /* Style for the dropdown menu */
2    select#cuisine {
3      width: 200px;
4      padding: 5px;
5      border: 1px solid #ccc;
6      border-radius: 5px;
7      font-size: 16px;
8      margin-bottom: 10px;
9    }
10
11   /* Style for the dropdown placeholder text */
12   select#cuisine::placeholder {
13     color: #999;
14   }
15
16   /* Style for the dropdown options */
17   select#cuisine option {
18     font-size: 16px;
```

```
19  }
20
21  /* style for the label */
22  .subheading {
23    display: block;
24    margin-top: 10px;
25    font-size: 16px;
26    font-weight: bold;
27    margin-bottom: 10px;
28  }
```

Getting the Cuisine into the Prompt

When the user clicks the submit button, it sends the chosen cuisine to our trusty **generate_recipe** function, much like it did for the ingredients. Inside the function of generate_recipe, we can extract the cuisine from the form data using the following code.

```
1  def generate_recipe():
2      ...
3      # Extract the cuisine
4      selected_cuisine = request.form.get('cuisine')
```

Once we have the chosen cuisine, we can then use the **selected_-cuisine** in our prompt:

```
1      if selected_cuisine:
2          prompt += f" The cuisine should be
3                           {selected_cuisine}."
```

Voila! With just a simple tweak to our application, we've unlocked a whole new dimension of culinary delight. Now you can effortlessly select the perfect cuisine to match your mood, all based on those three lone ingredients!

Adding Food Restrictions

Prepare to take control of your culinary destiny! We're introducing yet another dimension to your food adventure – the power to select dietary restrictions that accommodate your lifestyle. Whether it's gluten-free, dairy-free, or other culinary paths, we've got choices that cater to every preference. Get ready to savor the taste of individual freedom as our recipe app harnesses code to bring these culinary choices to life!

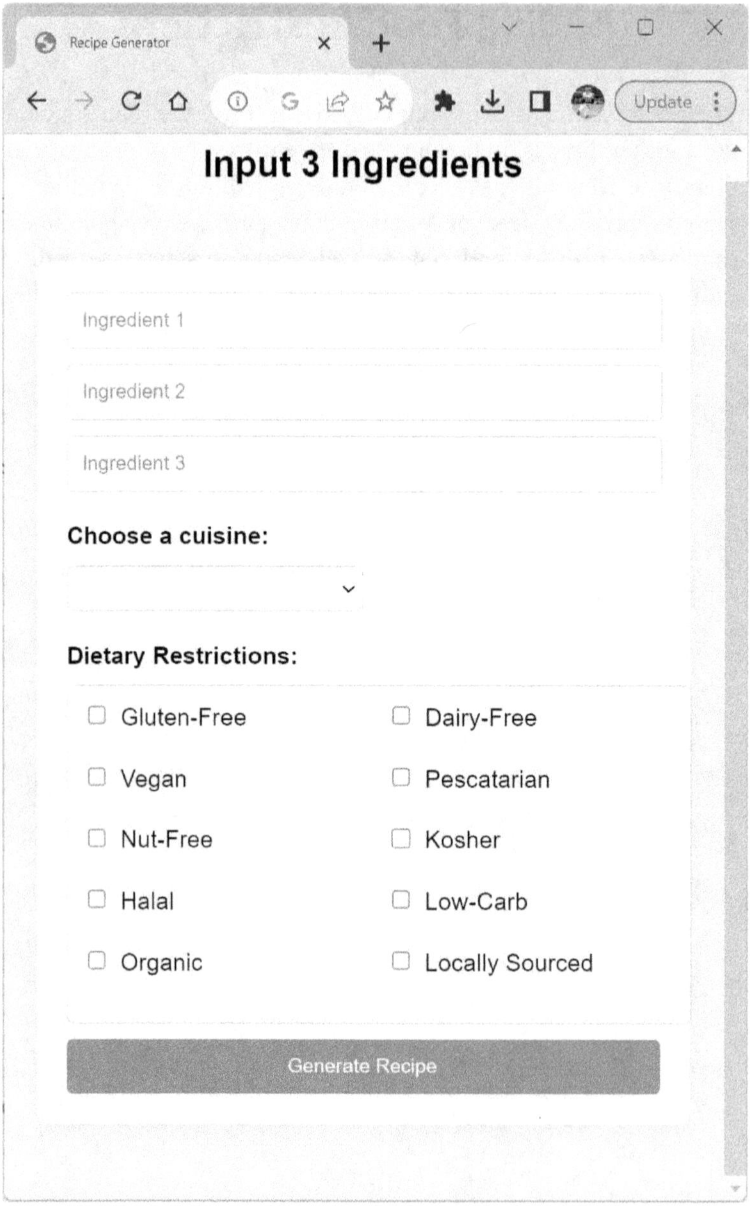

Figure 28. Food Restrictions

Populating the List of Food Restrictions

In order to get all our food restriction checkboxes into the form,
we first need to list them all in Python. Here is the restriction list
declared inside of **recipe.py**

```
1   dietary_restrictions = [
2       "Gluten-Free",
3       "Dairy-Free",
4       "Vegan",
5       "Pescatarian",
6       "Nut-Free",
7       "Kosher",
8       "Halal",
9       "Low-Carb",
10      "Organic",
11      "Locally Sourced",
12  ]
```

We can pass these dietary_restrictions into our **index.html** template the same way we passed the cuisine, through the render_-template function. We'll just modify render_template to also take the dietary_restrictions:

```
1   return render_template('index.html',
2           cuisines=cuisines,
3           dietary_restrictions=dietary_restrictions)
```

Inside of the index.html template, we'll use the power of Jinja2 to
loop through the dietary_restrictions and generate each checkbox
representing a restriction. Note: In the provided HTML code, all the
checkboxes have the same name attribute, which is restrictions.
This common name attribute serves a specific purpose: it allows
you to group these checkboxes together so that when the form is
submitted later, you can retrieve all the selected restrictions as a list
on the server side.

```
1   <label class="subheading" for="restrictions">Dietary
2           Restrictions:</label>
3       <div class="checkbox-container">
4         {% for restriction in dietary_restrictions %}
5         <div class="checkbox-group" name="restrictions">
6           <label class="checkbox-label">
7             <input
8               type="checkbox"
9               name="restrictions"
10              value="{{ restriction|lower|replace(
11                             ' ', '_') }}"
12            />
13            {{ restriction }}
14          </label>
15        </div>
16        {% endfor %}
17      </div>
```

Styling the Dietary Restrictions Checkboxes

We want to create two columns of restrictions instead of one long
column, so the restrictions fit better on the page. In order to do this
kind of layout, it's going to require that we take advantage of Flex.
Flex gives us the ability to organize our layout into a grid structure,
so our checkboxes align neatly into two columns:

```
1    /* Styling for a container to group checkboxes */
2    .checkbox-container {
3      border: 1px solid #ccc;
4      padding: 10px;
5      border-radius: 5px;
6      width: 400px;
7      margin-bottom: 10px;
8      display: flex;
9      flex-wrap: wrap;
10     justify-content: space-between;
11     max-width: 400px; /* Adjust the width as needed */
12   }
13
14   /* Style for the individual checkbox groups */
15   .checkbox-group {
16     flex: 0 0 calc(50% - 5px); /* 50% width with a
17                                   little margin in between */
18     margin-bottom: 10px; /* Space between groups */
19     display: flex;
20     align-items: center;
21   }
22
23   /* Styling for labels associated with checkboxes */
24   label.checkbox-label {
25     display: inline-block;
26     margin-right: 10px;
27   }
```

Below is the breakdown of what each css class does to give us the nicely aligned checkboxes

.checkbox-container: This class is applied to the outer ‹div›, creating a border around the checkboxes and defining the maximum width of the border. Additionally, it configures the flex layout to wrap its contents, which consist of a set of *checkbox-groups*. The following styles demonstrate how flex is utilized to align the checkbox-groups within:

- **display: flex**: This property transforms the container into a flex container preparing it for the alignment of the checkbox groups contained within.
- **flex-wrap: wrap**: When there isn't enough horizontal space, this property allows the checkboxes to neatly wrap onto a new line.
- **justify-content: space-between**: It evenly distributes space between the checkbox groups, pushing them as far apart as possible horizontally.
- **max-width**: Sets an upper limit on the container's width, capping it at 400px to ensure it won't exceed this width.

.checkbox-group: This class is used to style the `<div>` that contains the label-checkbox pair inside the `.checkbox-container`. The following properties dictate the alignment of these checkbox-groups:

- **flex: 0 0 calc(50% - 5px)**: This property controls the width of each checkbox group. With `flex` set to `0 0`, it prevents the width from growing or shrinking. The calculation `calc(50% - 5px)` results in a width of 50% of the container's width minus 5 pixels, creating a margin between checkbox groups. This design ensures that each checkbox group occupies 50% of the row width, allowing only two checkbox groups to fit on a single row.
- **display: flex**: This property transforms each checkbox group into a flex container itself, aiding in the alignment of the checkbox and its associated label.

These CSS rules work together harmoniously to create an organized and visually appealing layout for the checkboxes.

Getting Dietary Restriction into the Prompt

We've created the UI and are ready to ingest the feedback from the user/chef, so what steps do we need to take? First of all, we need to retrieve a list of the restrictions that have been checked by our discerning user. We can do this inside our **generate_recipe** method just like we retrieved the cuisine:

```
@app.route('/generate_recipe', methods=['POST'])
def generate_recipe():
    # Extract the three ingredients from the user's input
    ingredients = request.form.getlist('ingredient')

    # Extract cuisine and restrictions
    selected_cuisine = request.form.get('cuisine')
    selected_restrictions = request.form.getlist(
                            'restrictions')
```

The getlist method on the form will pull in all the restrictions that were checked. We can then go ahead and use the returned list directly in our prompt.

Getting the Dietary Restriction into the Prompt

In the same function, generate_recipe, we can add just a few lines of code to append any food restrictions that were checked by the user. We take advantage of the **join** function to turn the selected_restrictions list into a comma delimited string of restrictions:

```
1    if selected_restrictions and len(
2      selected_restrictions) > 0:
3        prompt += f" The recipe should have the
4                         following restrictions:
5
6      {', '.join(selected_restrictions)}."
```

Let's run the flask app:

```
1  flask --app recipe run
```

Running the flask web app produces the following window in the browser:

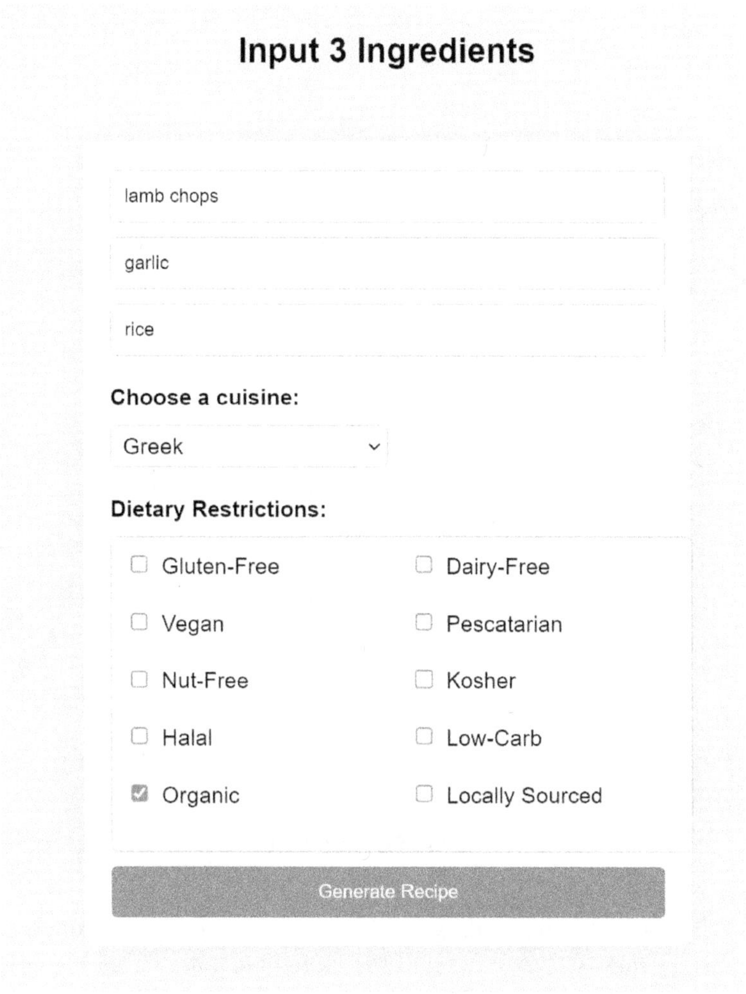

Input 3 Ingredients

lamb chops

garlic

rice

Choose a cuisine:

Greek ⌄

Dietary Restrictions:

☐ Gluten-Free   ☐ Dairy-Free

☐ Vegan   ☐ Pescatarian

☐ Nut-Free   ☐ Kosher

☐ Halal   ☐ Low-Carb

☑ Organic   ☐ Locally Sourced

Generate Recipe

Figure 29. Diet Restrictions in the App

Now, let's pick three ingredients and ask for a Greek cuisine with an organic restriction in place and click the Generate Recipe button. Below is the resulting recipe:

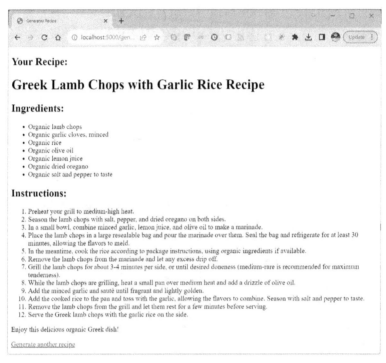

Figure 30. Recipe Generated in the Browser

Conclusion

Who knew coding could work up such an appetite? Throughout this journey, we've unearthed the incredible potential of blending simple Python and HTML with the advanced capabilities of the ChatGPT API. With just a handful of lines, we can create a fully functional website. The possibilities are endless: from personal assistants to content generators, and perhaps even novel applications we've yet to conceive, the horizon is now bursting with opportunities awaiting our creative touch. Let's use this newfound knowledge to shape the future of digital experiences!

Puzzle Book

Figure 31. Puzzle Image

Introduction

Our journey into the endless possiblities of ChatGPT now brings us to the world of puzzle games. We seamlessly blend AI tools with programming to generate a Word Search Book using ChatGPT! But this chapter is not just about puzzles; it's a creative endeavor

where we repurpose the user-friendly interface from our previous
storytelling Tkinter app to inspire a new product. Instead of
generating dialogues, ChatGPT will produce lists of thematic words
for our puzzles. Acting on a selected theme from a dropdown menu,
ChatGPT instantaneously delivers a set of words that Python then
meticulously arranges into puzzles. The words are hidden mas-
terfully with varied orientations. First we will guide you through
producing a PDF page with a puzzle and corresponding word list.
The final sections of the chapter will introduce techniques to batch
process multiple topics in a theme, allowing you to craft a complete
Word Search Book compiled neatly into a PDF. Hang on for the
ride—it's going to be fun!

Setting up the Virtual Environment

Run the following to set up your virtual environment:

```
1   python -m venv puzzlebook
```

and activate it:

```
1   .\puzzlebook\Scripts\activate
```

Also install all necessary libraries for this project:

```
1   pip install openai pillow requests
2                python-dotenv tk reportlab
```

Now let's get programming!

The User Interface

The UI we create will look very similar to the one in our storytelling application, but here we only need one drop down in order to pick the theme of our word search puzzle.

Figure 32. Word Search UI

Here is the UI layout code:

```
1   app = tk.Tk()
2   app.title("Word Puzzle Book")
3
4
5   # Label and ComboBox for the first animal
6   label1 = ttk.Label(app,
7               text="Select a Word Puzzle Theme:")
8   label1.grid(column=0, row=0, padx=10, pady=5)
9   combo1 = ttk.Combobox(
10      app, values=["Holidays", "Science", "Travel",
11      "AI", "Cars", "Food", "Entertainment",
```

```
12        "Sports", "Space", "Work", "School",
13        "Animals", "Nature", "Art", "Music",
14        "Movies", "Books", "History", "Math",
15        "Geography", "Weather", "Fashion",
16        "Health", "Family", "Money", "Politics",
17        "Religion", "Technology", "Games",
18        "Business", "Crime", "Law", "Medicine",              "Ps\
19   ychology", "Language", "Culture",
20        "Relationships", "Social Media", "News",
21        "Shopping", "Transportation",
22        "Architecture", "Design", "Gardening",
23        "Hobbies", "Humor", "Literature",
24        "Philosophy", "Photography", "Writing",
25        "Other"])
26
27   combo1.grid(column=1, row=0, padx=10, pady=5)
28   combo1.set("Holidays")
29
30
31   # Button to submit the details
32   submit_btn = ttk.Button(app, text="Submit",
33                            command=submit)
34   submit_btn.grid(column=1, row=3, padx=10, pady=20)
35
36   # make it scrollable
37   # Create a Scrollbar widget
38   scrollbar = tk.Scrollbar(app)
39   scrollbar.grid(row=4, column=3, sticky='ns')
40
41   # Text widget to display results
42   result_text = tk.Text(app, width=50, height=10,
43                    wrap=tk.WORD,
44                    yscrollcommand=scrollbar.set)
45   result_text.grid(column=0, row=4, columnspan=2,
46                    padx=10, pady=10)
```

```
47   result_text.config(state="disabled")
48
49   image_holder = tk.Label(app)
50   image_holder.grid(column=0, row=5,
51           columnspan=4, padx=10, pady=10)
52
53   puzzle_holder = tk.Label(app)
54   puzzle_holder.grid(column=5, row=0, rowspan=6,
55                       padx=2,  pady=2)
56
57   label_key_title = ttk.Label(app, text=
58                           "Puzzle Words")
59   label_key_title.grid(column=5, row=6, padx=10, pady=5)
60
61   label_puzzle_words = ttk.Label(app, text="")
62   label_puzzle_words.grid(column=5, row=7, padx=10, pady=10)
63
64   # Button to submit the details
65   create_pdf_btn = ttk.Button(
66       app, text="Create Pdf",
67       command=lambda: create_pdf(
68           label_puzzle_words['text']))
69   create_pdf_btn.grid(column=2, row=3,
70                       padx=10,pady=20)
71
72   scrollbar.config(command=result_text.yview)
73
74   # Link the scrollbar to the text widget (so the scrollbar\
75    knows how to scroll the text widget)
76
77   app.mainloop()
```

Notice we've added a few additional labels: label_puzzle_words will contain the list of words we are searching for in the puzzle. puzzle_holder will hold an image of our word search puzzle. Clicking the submit_btn will initiate the process of generating the word puzzle and displaying it in our UI.

Let's take a look at the submit event handler:

```
1   def submit():
2       set_wait_cursor()
3       theme = combo1.get()
4
5       prompt
6         = f"Create a comma delimited list of 40
7         words having to do with the theme {theme}.
8         None of the words in the list should
9         repeat\n"
10      messages = [{'role': 'user', 'content':
11                  prompt}]
12      # get a list of 40 related words from
13      # chat gpt
14      response = openai.ChatCompletion.create(
15          model="gpt-3.5-turbo",
16          messages=messages,
17          temperature=0.8,
18          top_p=1.0,
19          frequency_penalty=0.0,
20          presence_penalty=0.6,
21      )
22
23      print(prompt)
24
25      # retrieve the list of words created by ChatGPT
26      chatGPTAnswer =
27        response["choices"][0]["message"]
28                  ["content"]
29      print(chatGPTAnswer)
30      # split the comma delimited
31      # list of words into a list
32      words = chatGPTAnswer.split(',')
```

```
33    # pick out a list of 10 viable words
34    words = clean_words(words)
35    print(words)
36    # create word search puzzle array from words
37    (board, words_to_remove) = puzzle_board_creator
38                           .create_word_search(words)
39    # remove words that could not be placed
40    words = [word for word in words
41                   if word not in words_to_remove]
42    # show the board on the console
43    puzzle_board_creator.display_board(board)
44    label_puzzle_words.config(text=', '.join(words))
45    # make result_text scrollable
46
47    result_text.config(state="normal")
48    # Clear any previous results
49    result_text.delete(1.0, tk.END)
50    result_text.insert(tk.END, chatGPTAnswer)
51    result_text.config(state="disabled")
52
53    # generates a cartoon image of the theme
54    image_url = generate_image(theme)
55    # creates a grid of letters into
56    # an image for the puzzle
57    create_grid_of_letters_image(board)
58     # display theme image
59    display_image_from_url(image_holder, image_url)
60    # display puzzle image
61    display_image_from_path(puzzle_holder,
62                puzzle_image_path)
63    puzzle_holder.config(width=600, height=600)
64    set_normal_cursor()
```

This submit method is a significant function within our application that facilitates the generation of a word search puzzle based on a selected theme. Below is a step-by-step explanation of what each segment of the submit method does:

Explanation

The submit method generates the word search puzzle when the user clicks the submit button. Here's a breakdown of its functionality:

1. **set_wait_cursor()**: Changes the cursor to a waiting state, indicating that a process is underway.

2. **theme = combo1.get()**: Retrieves the user-selected theme from a ComboBox widget (combo1).

   - Constructs a prompt requesting ChatGPT to create a list of 40 unique words, separate by commas, related to the chosen theme.

   - Sends this prompt to OpenAI's GPT-3.5 Turbo via the openai.ChatCompletion.create method and obtains a response.

4. **Extract & Process ChatGPT's Response:**

   - Extracts and prints the list of words from ChatGPT's response.

5. **Puzzle Creation & Word Removal:**

   - Calls puzzle_board_creator.create_word_search(words) to generate a puzzle board with the selected words. We'll be dedicating part of this chapter to explaining more about the PuzzleBoardCreator class.

6. **Puzzle Board Display & Label Update:**

```
1    puzzle_board_creator.display_board(board)
2    label_puzzle_words.config(text=', '.join(words))
```

- Calls `puzzle_board_creator.display_board` to print the puzzle board to the console for debugging purposes.

7. Text Widget Update:

```
1        result_text.config(state="normal")
2        # Clear any previous results
3        result_text.delete(1.0, tk.END)
4        result_text.insert(tk.END, chatGPTAnswer)
5        result_text.config(state="disabled")
```

- Enables, clears, updates with ChatGPT's response, and disables the `result_text` Tkinter Text widget so it can't be edited.

8. Image Generation & Display:

```
1        # generates a cartoon image of the theme
2        image_url = generate_image(theme)
3        # creates a grid of letters into an
4        # image for the puzzle
5        create_grid_of_letters_image(board)
6        # display the theme image
7        display_image_from_url(image_holder,
8                                    image_url)
9        # display the puzzle image
10       display_image_from_path(puzzle_holder,
11                                   puzzle_image_path)
12       # resize the puzzle label
13       puzzle_holder.config(width=600,
14                                   height=600)
```

- generate_image(theme) creates and returns a URL of a cartoon image representing the theme generated by DALLE. Here is the generate_image function which calls openai to get the image from our prompt (almost identical to the same function used in storytelling in Chapter 2 except the prompt is different):

```
1    # retrieve the temporary url which
2    # has a link to the generated image
3    image_url = response.data[0]["url"]
4    print(image_url)
5    return image_url
6    ```
```

- create_grid_of_letters_image(board) generates a puzzle image out of the letter grid. It uses the pillow library to create an initial 530x530 pixel white board and then proceeds to step through each letter in the letter board matrix and places it onto the image in the proper position. We'll be going over this function later in the chapter when we discuss the puzzle creation.

- display_image_from_url displays the theme image generated by DALLE. This is similar to the code we used in our storytelling app in Chapter 2 to display the animal story image.

```
1   def display_image_from_url(image_holder, url):
2       # Fetch the image from the URL
3       response = requests.get(url)
4       image_data = BytesIO(response.content)
5
6       # Open and display the image
7       # using PIL and tkinter
8       image = Image.open(image_data)
9       image.resize((200, 200), Image.ANTIALIAS)
10
11      # Save the image as a PNG
12      image.save(pil_image_path, "PNG")
13
14      photo = ImageTk.PhotoImage(image)
15
16      update_label_with_new_image(image_holder,
17                                  photo)
18      return image
```

- display_image_from_path displays the puzzle image on a label widget, adjusting the puzzle_holder widget's dimensions to fit the grid of letters. This function is discussed in detail later in this chapter.

9. set_normal_cursor(): Reverts the cursor back to its normal state, signaling the end of the process.

```
1   def set_normal_cursor():
2       submit_btn.config(cursor="")
```

Summary:

The submit method automates the end-to-end process of generating a themed word search puzzle. It captures the user's theme choice, solicits ChatGPT for relevant words, creates a puzzle with these words, and updates the GUI with the puzzle, word list, and associated images. This function is central to the interactive experience of generating and displaying word puzzles in the application.

The Puzzle Board Creator Class

In the submit code we've got a pretty good idea of how we can use ChatGPT to create a themed list. We simply set the prompt and call the API. What is not as apparent is how we take the next step and generate a word puzzle out of the list returned to us. To create the word puzzle, we've written a specialized class called PuzzleBoardCreator that takes that themed list of words and systematically inserts those words into a 13x13 array. The words can be inserted vertically, horizontally, and diagonally starting from any direction (bottom-to-top, top-to-bottom, left-to-right, or right-to-left), which makes the puzzle more challenging. In this next section, we'll explore the algorithm that populates the words randomly on the board.

The place_word method

Inside our PuzzleBoardCreator, we have a method called place_word which does all the work in placing an individual word on the board. The method place_word takes 2 parameters: board representing the grid of letters and word the word we are placing onto the board. The clean_word method strips out any punctuation or spaces since we can't really have them in a word search puzzle.

```
1    def clean_word(self, word):
2        word = word.upper().replace(" ", "")
3        # remove any punctuation
4        word = word.translate(
5                str.maketrans('',
6                '', string.punctuation))
7        return word
```

The algorithm for placing words in the puzzle is illustrated in the following flowchart diagram:

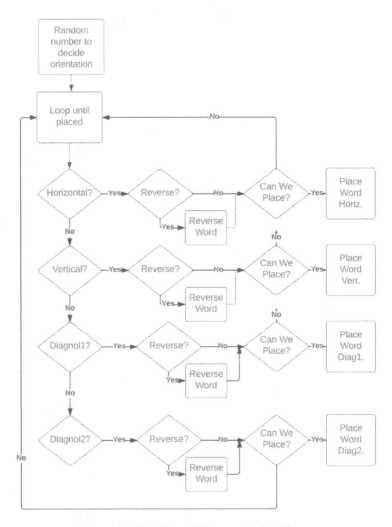

Figure 33. Word Search Placement Algorithm

Basically, we are randomly placing a word in the puzzle in a random orientation with a random letter direction in a random row and column. If the algorithm cannot place the word it keeps trying with new random positions. Here is the flowchart algorithm converted to code.

```
 1  def place_word(self, board, word):
 2    print("placing word: " + word)
 3    # keep it at 10 characters
 4    word = self.clean_word(word)
 5    # Randomly choose orientation: 0=horizontal,
 6    # 1=vertical, 2=diagonal
 7    orientation = random.randint(0, 3)
 8    placed = False
 9    count = 0
10    while not placed:
11      count += 1
12      if count > 200000:
13          print("count exceeded {count}"
14              .format(count=count))
15          return placed
16
17      if orientation == 0:  # Horizontal
18          row = random.randint(0, len(board)-1)
19          col = random.randint(0, len(board)
20                                  -len(word))
21          reverse = random.choice([True, False])
22          if reverse:
23              word = word[::-1]
24          space_available = all(
25              board[row][c] == '-' or
26              board[row][c] == word[i]
27              for i, c in enumerate(
28                  range(col, col+len(word)))
29              )
30
31          if space_available:
32              for i, c in enumerate(
33                  range(col, col+len(word))):
34                  board[row][c] = word[i]
35              placed = True
```

```
36
37     elif orientation == 1:  # Vertical
38         row = random.randint(0, len(board)
39                                 -len(word))
40         col = random.randint(0, len(board)-1)
41         reverse = random.choice([True, False])
42         if reverse:
43             word = word[::-1]
44         space_available =
45             all(board[r][col] == '-' or
46             board[r][col] == word[i]
47                 for i, r in enumerate(          \
48             range(row, row+len(word)))
49                 )
50         if space_available:
51             for i, r in
52                 enumerate(range(row,            \
53                 row+len(word))):
54                 board[r][col] = word[i]
55             placed = True
56     # Diagonal top-left to bottom right
57     elif orientation == 2:
58         row = random.randint(0, len(board)
59                 -len(word))
60         col = random.randint(0, len(board)
61                                 -len(word))
62         reverse = random.choice([True, False])
63         if reverse:
64             word = word[::-1]
65         space_available = all(
66             board[r][c] == '-'
67             or
68             board[r][c] == word[i]
69             for i, (r, c) in enumerate(
70             zip(range(row, row+len(word)),
```

```
71              range(col, col+len(word))))))
72          if space_available:
73              for i, (r, c) in enumerate(
74                  zip(range(row, row+len(word)),
75                  range(col, col+len(word)))):
76                  board[r][c] = word[i]
77              placed = True
78      # Diagonal bottom-left to top-right
79      elif orientation == 3:
80          row = random.randint(len(word) - 1,
81              len(board) - 1)
82          col = random.randint(0,
83              len(board) - len(word))
84          reverse = random.choice([True, False])
85          if reverse:
86              word = word[::-1]
87          space_available = all(
88              board[r][c] == '-' or
89              board[r][c] == word[i]
90              for i, (r, c) in
91                      enumerate(zip(range(row,
92                          row-len(word), -1),
93                          range(col,
94                          col+len(word)))))
95          if space_available:
96              for i, (r, c) in
97                  enumerate(zip(range(row,
98                      row-len(word), -1),
99                      range(col, col+len(word)))):
100                  board[r][c] = word[i]
101              placed = True
102
103  return placed
```

Each orientation (horizontal, vertical, diagonal1 and diagonal2) is represented by an integer 0-3. The algorithm randomly generates a number 0 to 3 and follows the code designated by the particular matching orientation. Then the algorithm randomly generates whether to reverse the word or not. Once that decision is made, the code randomly selects a starting position (row and column) on the board where the word can be placed based on the orientation and length of the word. The algorithm checks if there's enough space available to place the word at the selected position without going out of the board's boundaries and without conflicting with any previously placed words. If the space is available, it checks if each character of the word either matches a character already present on the board or if the board's cell is empty (represented by '-'). If all these conditions are met, the word is placed on the board, and the placed variable is set to True, thereby exiting the while loop. However, if the conditions are not met, the while loop continues, attempting to place the word again with new randomly generated orientation, reverse status, and starting position, until the word is successfully placed or until the count of attempts exceeds 200,000. In the latter case, the function returns False, indicating that the word couldn't be placed on the board.

Filling the Empty Spaces

Once we've placed all the words on the board, we'll want to fill in the rest of the board with empty spaces. The `fill_empty` method does just that by filling in all unoccupied `board` elements with a random letter of the alphabet:

```
1    def fill_empty(self, board):
2        for row in range(len(board)):
3            for col in range(len(board)):
4                if board[row][col] == '-':
5                    board[row][col] =
6                        random.choice(
7                            string.
8                            ascii_uppercase)
```

Putting it all Together

Now that we have all the methods we need to fill in the board, we can create an overall method that takes a list of puzzle words, places them on the board, and then fills the gaps in the board as well. Below is our create_word_search method that does all the work. Note: If we can't place a word for some reason, we add it to a remove word list, which we later use to strip those words from the list.

```
1    def create_word_search(self, words):
2        words_to_remove = []
3        board = [['-' for _ in range(13)]
4            for _ in range(13)]
5
6        # go through the list of words and
7        # try to place each word on the board
8        for word in words:
9            placed = self.place_word(board, word)
10           if (not placed):
11               words_to_remove.append(word)
12
13       # fill in the missing letter gaps
14       # on the board
15       self.fill_empty(board)
```

16
```
17        return (board, words_to_remove)
```

Putting the Puzzle into a Graphic File

As in the Storytelling Chapter, we will once again take advantage of the Python Pillow library to generate and save an image of a 13 by 13 grid of letters. The Pillow library allows for extensive manipulation of images, including creating new images, drawing on them, and saving them in various formats. Within the function, `Image.new('RGB', img_size, background_color)` initializes a new image with the specified size img_size (650 by 650 pixels) and white background color `background_color`. The `ImageDraw.Draw(img)` creates a drawable image, allowing letters to be placed onto it.

The function attempts to use a TrueType font located at the specified path ('C:\Windows\Fonts\Cour.ttf'), setting it to the defined font_size of 30. In case the font is not found (triggering an IOError), a message is printed to the console, and the function reverts to using the default system font through ImageFont.load_default(). The Cour.ttf font, which belongs to the Courier font family, is utilized in this function because it is a monospaced font where each character occupies the same horizontal width, ensuring a uniform and aligned grid of letters in the generated image. This is in contrast to proportional fonts like Arial, where the width of characters can vary, leading to misalignment and inconsistency in the visual presentation of the letter grid.

The code proceeds by iterating over the 13 by 13 letters input array to populate the grid on the image. The positioning of each letter is adjusted and calculated based on the index of the loop and the predefined font_size plus an additional 10 pixels to ensure proper spacing. Each letter from the letters array is drawn onto the image in black color (0, 0, 0). Finally, the completed image is saved to the file path specified by the puzzle_image_path variable, which should be a string representing a valid path to a .png file where the image will be stored. Ensure you have the appropriate write permissions at the location specified by puzzle_image_path for the image-saving operation to succeed.

```
1   from PIL import Image, ImageTk, ImageDraw, ImageFont
2
3   def create_grid_of_letters_image(letters):
4       # Set image size, background color, and font size
5       img_size = (650, 650)
6       background_color = (255, 255, 255)  # white
7       font_size = 30
8
9       # Create a new image with white background
10      img = Image.new('RGB', img_size,
11                          background_color)
12      d = ImageDraw.Draw(img)
13
14      # Load a truetype or OpenType font file,
15      # and set the font size
16      try:
17          fnt = ImageFont.truetype(
18              'C:\\Windows\\Fonts\\Cour.ttf',
19                          font_size)
20      except IOError:
21          print('Font not found,
22                  using default font.')
23          fnt = ImageFont.load_default()
24
25      # Generate the 13 by 13 grid of letters
26
27      for i in range(13):
28          for j in range(13):
29              # Cycle through the puzzle letters
30              letter = letters[i][j]
```

```
31              # Adjust position for each letter
32              position = (j * (font_size + 10)
33                          + 75,
34               i * (font_size + 10) + 75)
35              # Draw letter with black color
36              d.text(position, letter, font=fnt,
37                      fill=(0, 0, 0))
38
39      # Save the image to a png file
40      img.save(puzzle_image_path)
```

Once we've called `create_grid_of_letters_image` function, we'll want to place the image in a label control in Tk so we can view it in our application. The display_image_from_path function will do that for us. The function takes the parameters of a Tk label image and a png file path and uses these to fill the Tk label with the image we generated for the puzzle. The auxiliary function, `update_label_with_new_image` is used to place the Tk PhotoImage from memory into the label:

```
1   def display_image_from_path(image_holder, path):
2       # Fetch the image from the file
3
4       # open image from path
5       # 'c:\\temp\\alphabet_grid.png'
6       image = Image.open(path)
7
8       # convert the png to a photo image
9       # which can be used by Tk
10      # to display the image
11      photo = ImageTk.PhotoImage(image)
12
13      update_label_with_new_image(image_holder,
14                                  photo)
15      return image
```

```
16
17   def update_label_with_new_image(label, photo):
18       label.config(image=photo)
19       # Keep a reference to avoid
20       # garbage collection
21       label.image = photo
```

Results from Submit

Let's see what happens when we run the app, choose a category, and hit the submit button:

You can run the app from the command line by typing:

```
1    python -m PuzzleBook.py
```

This will bring up the initial screen:

Figure 34. Running the Application

We'll choose the default category, Holidays, as our category to create the puzzle. Now let's click the submit button:

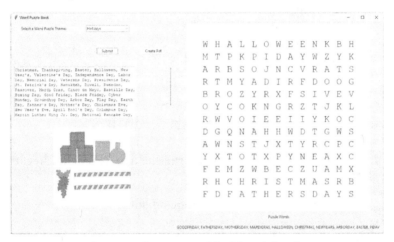

Figure 35. Generating a Word Search Puzzle

The resulting screen shows all of the holidays generated by Chat-GPT in the results text box. It also generated a holiday image using DALLE (much as we did in the storytelling chapter). On the right side of the application it generated a word search puzzle for the ten chosen Holidays listed below the puzzle. We've taken the first step in creating our word search book! The next step is to get our initial puzzle into a PDF.

Creating the PDF

The `create_pdf(puzzle_word_text)` function in the provided Python code is designed to generate a PDF document, incorporating images and text related to a puzzle. Initially, the function checks if the `puzzle_word_text` parameter is not empty; if it is empty, an error message is displayed prompting the user to generate dialog first, and the function terminates. The code extracts a theme from a combo box (assumed GUI element) named `combo1`. Subsequently, it initializes a PDF document using the SimpleDocTemplate class from the reportlab library, setting its page size to a letter. The PDF content is constructed by appending a headline (derived from the selected theme and styled with Heading1), two images (whose paths are specified by pil_image_path and puzzle_image_path, and dimensions are set to 2.5x2.5 and 5x5 inches respectively), and formatted puzzle_word_text as a paragraph. The puzzle_word_text is formatted to replace newline characters with appropriate HTML line-break tags for proper display in the PDF. Finally, the doc.build(contents) statement compiles and saves the PDF with the arranged contents.

```
1   def create_pdf(puzzle_word_text):
2       if not puzzle_word_text:
3           messagebox.showerror("Error", "Please
4                   generate the dialog first!")
5           return
6
7       theme = combo1.get()
8
9       # Create a PDF with both the extracted
10      # image and some text
11      doc = SimpleDocTemplate("output.pdf",
12                  pagesize=letter)
13
14      # Create the contents list for the PDF
15      contents = []
16
17      styles = getSampleStyleSheet()
18      headline_style = styles['Heading1']
19      headline = Paragraph(theme.capitalize(),
20                  headline_style)
21      contents.append(headline)
22
23      # Add the extracted theme image
```

```
24    # Adjust width and height as needed
25    img1 = ReportLabImage(pil_image_path,
26            width=2.5*inch, height=2.5*inch)
27    contents.append(img1)
28
29    # Add the puzzle image
30    img2 = ReportLabImage(puzzle_image_path,
31            width=5*inch, height=5*inch)
32    contents.append(img2)
33
34    # Add the puzzle words
35    puzzle_word_text = '<br/>' + puzzle_word_text
36    puzzle_word_text = puzzle_word_text.replace(
37                       '\n', '<br/><br/>')
38    styles = getSampleStyleSheet()
39    paragraph = Paragraph(puzzle_word_text,
40                          styles['Normal'])
41    contents.append(paragraph)
42
43    # Build the PDF
44    doc.build(contents)
```

When we hit the create pdf button, it runs the `create_pdf` function above and compiles together the theme name, the generated theme picture, the puzzle and the list of puzzle words into output.pdf and it produces the single page puzzle sheet shown below.

Holidays

```
W H A L L O W E E N K B H
M T P K P I D A Y W Z Y K
A R B S O J N C V R A T S
R T M Y A D I R F D O O G
B R O Z Y R X F S I V E V
O Y C O K N G R Z T J K L
R W V O I E E I I Y K O C
D G Q N A H H W D T G W S
A W N S T J X T Y R C P C
Y X T O T X P Y N E A X C
F E M Z W B E C Z U A M X
R H C H R I S T M A S R B
F D F A T H E R S D A Y S
```

GOODFRIDAY, FATHERSDAY, MOTHERSDAY, MARDIGRAS, HALLOWEEN, CHRISTMAS,
NEWYEARS, ARBORDAY, EASTER, PIDAY

Figure 36. Word Search in a pdf file

Creating an Entire Book

We now have all the pieces available to create an entire word search book. What we'll do is use the strategy of two levels of indirection. We'll use ChatGPT to generate a list of 10 topics from our theme and then we'll take those 10 topics and produce 10 puzzles, a puzzle on each page of the book. Note this can easily be scaled out to 100 pages by asking ChatGPT for more topics, but we'll keep it small for the purpose of understanding how this can all be done.

Creating a `batch_submit` Function

The goal of this project is to ultimately create a 10-page puzzle book based on a particular theme. We'll pick the theme from the dropdown, but after that, we'll use ChatGPT to produce topics from that theme. Then we'll loop through the topics and create puzzles. We've already written all the code for doing the puzzle creation, we just need to save the path of each puzzle image as we progress, as well as the path of the theme image, and the list of puzzle words. The strategy here will be to have three arrays that will remember everything we generate. When we are finished generating all the components of every page of our books, we'll send the whole thing to a `create_book` function which will produce our entire book in a pdf file. The book will be complete with page numbers as well as the topic of the theme listed in the header.

As stated, the `batch_submit` function is designed to automate the process of generating word search puzzles based on themes and to compile these into a book. Below is a step-by-step explanation of what the function does:

Initialization: Initializes empty lists to store words for puzzles, images related to themes, images of puzzles, and puzzle descriptions.

Fetching Theme: Sets a wait cursor (indicating a loading state in the UI), retrieves a selected theme from the combo box, and constructs a prompt to request a list of 40 words related to this theme.

First OpenAI Call: Sends a message to OpenAI's GPT-3.5 Turbo with the constructed prompt to get a comma-delimited list of 40 words related to the initial theme.

Words Retrieval and Cleaning: Retrieves and prints the response, then splits and cleans it into a list of words (topics). Only 10 cleaned, viable words are selected from this list.

Iterative Puzzle Creation: For each topic in the cleaned list:

Saving Description: Saves the current topic as a puzzle description. Subsequent OpenAI Calls: Constructs a new prompt with the current topic and gets a new list of 40 words related to this topic using another OpenAI call.

Words Processing: Retrieves, splits, cleans, and selects words from the response, creating and displaying a word search puzzle with these words, and updating the UI elements with the retrieved words and created puzzle.

Image Generation and Display: Generates and displays images related to the current topic, copying them to specific paths and storing these paths in the lists initialized earlier.

Book Creation: After iterating through all topics, calls the create_book function with the lists of words, theme images, puzzle images, and puzzle descriptions as arguments to compile and generate a book of word search puzzles.

Summary: batch_submit automates the process of creating word search puzzles. For a given theme, it fetches related words using OpenAI, generates word search puzzles, retrieves and stores images for each puzzle and theme, and finally compiles these elements into a book. Each step involves interactions with the user interface, file system, and OpenAI's GPT-3.5 Turbo API.

```
1   def batch_submit():
2       puzzle_words_list = []
3       theme_images_list = []
4       puzzle_images_list = []
5       puzzle_descriptions = []
6
7       set_wait_cursor()
8       theme = combo1.get()
9
10      prompt = f"Create a comma delimited \
11              list of 40 words having to do \
12              with the theme {theme}. None of \
13              the words in the list \
14              should repeat\n"
15
16      messages = [{'role': 'user',
17                  'content': prompt}]
18
19      response = openai.ChatCompletion.create(
20          model="gpt-3.5-turbo",
21          messages=messages,
22          temperature=0.8,
23          top_p=1.0,
24          frequency_penalty=0.0,
25          presence_penalty=0.6,
26      )
27
28      print(prompt)
29
30      # retrieve the list of words
31      # created by ChatGPT
32      chatGPTAnswer
33      = response["choices"][0]["message"]
34                              ["content"]
35      print(chatGPTAnswer)
```

```
36      # split the comma delimited list
37      # of words into a list
38      topics = chatGPTAnswer.split(',')
39      # pick out a list of 10 viable words
40      topics = clean_words(topics)
41      print(topics)
42
43      # now create a list of words
44      # from each of those words
45      for topic in topics:
46          print(topic)
47          # save puzzle description
48          puzzle_descriptions.append(topic)
49
50          prompt
51            = f"Create a comma delimited list of
52              40 words having to do with the theme
53              {topic}. None of the words in the
54              list should repeat\n"
55          messages = [{'role': 'user', 'content':
56                              prompt}]
57          response = openai.ChatCompletion.create(
58              model="gpt-3.5-turbo",
59              messages=messages,
60              temperature=0.8,
61              top_p=1.0,
62              frequency_penalty=0.0,
63              presence_penalty=0.6,
64          )
65
66          print(prompt)
67
68          # retrieve the list of words created
69          # by ChatGPT
70          chatGPTAnswer
```

```
71              = response["choices"][0]["message"]
72                      ["content"]
73          print(chatGPTAnswer)
74          # split the comma delimited
75          # list of words into a list
76          words = chatGPTAnswer.split(',')
77          # pick out a list of 10 viable words
78          words = clean_words(words)
79          print(words)
80
81          # create word search puzzle array
82          # from words
83          (board, words_to_remove) =
84              puzzle_board_creator
85                .create_word_search(words)
86          # remove words that could not be placed
87          words = [word for word in words
88                      if word not in
89                        words_to_remove]
90          puzzle_words_list
91             .append(', '.join(words))
92          # show the board on the console
93          puzzle_board_creator.display_board(board)
94          label_puzzle_words.config(text=',
95                                    '.join(words))
96          # make result_text scrollable
97          result_text.config(state="normal")
98
99          # Clear any previous results
100         # and insert the new result
101         result_text.delete(1.0, tk.END)
102         result_text.insert(tk.END, chatGPTAnswer)
103         result_text.config(state="disabled")
104
105         # generates a cartoon image of the theme
```

```
106            image_url = generate_image(topic)
107
108            # creates a grid of letters into an
109            # image for the puzzle
110            create_grid_of_letters_image(board)
111
112            # add topic image to the
113            # topic image list
114            display_image_from_url(image_holder,
115                                   image_url)
116            dest_theme_image_path =
117              copy_image(pil_image_path, topic)
118            theme_images_list
119              .append(dest_theme_image_path)
120
121            # add puzzle image to puzzle image list
122            display_image_from_path(puzzle_holder,
123                                    puzzle_image_path)
124            dest_puzzle_image_path = copy_image
125                         (puzzle_image_path, topic)
126            puzzle_images_list.append
127                         (dest_puzzle_image_path)
128
129            puzzle_holder.config(width=600,
130                 height=600)
131            set_normal_cursor()
132
133        # create entire book into a pdf
134        create_book(puzzle_words_list,
135                    theme_images_list,
136                    puzzle_images_list,
137                    puzzle_descriptions)
```

Once we've collected batches of topic images, puzzle images, and puzzle key lists, we have everything we need to create our book.

Creating the Book

The batch_submit function concludes by calling create_book with generated content. create_book iteratively forms pages using the content at corresponding indices from four arrays: puzzle_-word_list, theme_images_list, puzzle_image_list, and puzzle_-descriptions. These arrays respectively contain puzzle topics, related images, puzzle images, and keywords to be found in each puzzle. The function processes these inputs to create a PDF book of word search puzzles, each page showcasing a distinct puzzle with its related content. Below is a breakdown of the create_book method:

1. **Initial Validation**: It first checks if any of the input lists are empty and whether all lists are of the same length. If not, it shows an error message and exits the function.

4. **PDF Generation**: After looping through all sets, it builds and saves the PDF document. If successful, it shows a success message. If an error occurs during this process, it catches the exception and displays an error message.

In essence, the function is creating a PDF book where each page is dedicated to a word search puzzle with its associated images and words, formatted and organized neatly for the reader.

```
1    from reportlab.platypus import
2        SimpleDocTemplate,
3        Paragraph, Image as ReportLabImage,
4        PageBreak,
5        Spacer, Table, TableStyle
6
7    def create_book(puzzle_words_list,
8                    theme_images_list,
9                    puzzle_images_list,
10                   puzzle_descriptions):
11       try:
12           print("creating the book...")
13           if not all([puzzle_words_list,
14             theme_images_list, puzzle_images_list,
15             puzzle_descriptions]):
16             messagebox.showerror(
17                 "Error",
18                 "Please provide non-empty lists \
19                 of puzzle words, \
20                 theme images, puzzle images, \
21                 and puzzle descriptions!")
22               return
23
24           if not len(puzzle_words_list) ==
25                   len(theme_images_list) ==
26                   len(puzzle_images_list) ==
27                   len(puzzle_descriptions):
28             messagebox.showerror(
29                 "Error",
30                 "All input lists must be \
31                  of the same length!")
32               return
33
34           # prepare the 6x9 template
35           custom_page_size = (6*72, 9*72)
```

```
36        custom_margins = 0.5*72
37        doc = SimpleDocTemplate("output.pdf",
38                 pagesize=custom_page_size,
39                 topMargin=custom_margins,
40                 bottomMargin=custom_margins,
41                 leftMargin=custom_margins,
42                 rightMargin=custom_margins)
43
44        styles = getSampleStyleSheet()
45        contents = []
46
47        headline_style = styles['Heading1']
48        normal_style = styles['Normal']
49
50        for i in range(len(puzzle_words_list)):
51            header_data = [[Paragraph(f"
52            {puzzle_descriptions[i]}",
53                            styles['Normal']),
54            Paragraph(f"{i + 1}",
55                    styles['Normal'])]]
56
57            # Create a table for the header with
58            # spacer on the left, topic in the
59            # middle, and page number
60            # on the right
61            margin_offset = 1*72
62            header_data = [['',
63
64                Paragraph(f"Topic: {
65                    puzzle_descriptions[i]}",
66                    styles['Normal']),
67
68                Paragraph(f"Page {i + 1}",
69                        styles['Normal'])]]
70
```

```
71          header_table = Table
72             (header_data,
73              colWidths = [
74                      margin_offset, 4*72,
75                      2*72
76                      ]
77              )
78
79          header_table.setStyle(
80             TableStyle([
81                ('ALIGN', (1, 0),
82                (2, 0), 'RIGHT'),
83                  ])
84              )
85
86          contents.append(header_table)
87          # Add some space between header
88          # and content
89          contents.append(Spacer(1, .5*72))
90
91          img1 = ReportLabImage(
92              theme_images_list[i],
93              width=1.5*inch, height=1.5*inch)
94          contents.append(img1)
95
96          contents.append(Spacer(1, .25*72))
97
98          img2 = ReportLabImage(
99              puzzle_images_list[i],
100             width=4*inch,
101             height=4*inch)
102         contents.append(img2)
103
104         contents.append(Spacer(1, .25*72))
105
```

```
106            puzzle_word_text = '<br/>' +
107                    puzzle_words_list[i]
108            puzzle_word_text = puzzle_word_text
109                .replace('\n', '<br/><br/>')
110            paragraph = Paragraph(
111                puzzle_word_text,
112                normal_style)
113            contents.append(paragraph)
114
115            # add page breaks at the end
116            # of the page
117            # if we are not on the last page
118            if i < len(puzzle_words_list) - 1:
119                contents.append(PageBreak())
120
121        # compile the contents into a pdf
122        doc.build(contents)
123        messagebox.showinfo("PDF Created",
124                "PDF created successfully!")
125    except Exception as e:
126        messagebox.showerror("Error",
127                f"Error creating PDF: {e}")
```

Adding a button to the UI

The only remaining task is to add a way to call batch_submit so we can create our book. Here we simply add a new button after the submit button called "create book". We also needed to adjust the layout a bit to get everything to line up properly:

```
1   app = tk.Tk()
2   app.title("Word Puzzle Book")
3
4
5   # Label and ComboBox for the first animal
6   label1 = ttk.Label(app, text=
7   "Select a Word Puzzle \
8                         Theme:")
9   label1.grid(column=0, row=0, padx=10, pady=5)
10  combo1 = ttk.Combobox(
11      app, values=["Holidays", "Science", "Travel",
12       "AI", "Cars", "Food", "Entertainment",
13       "Sports", "Space", "Work", "School",
14       "Animals", "Nature", "Art", "Music",
15       "Movies", "Books", "History", "Math",
16       "Geography", "Weather", "Fashion",
17       "Health", "Family", "Money",
18       "Politics", "Religion",
19       "Technology", "Games",
20       "Business", "Crime", "Law", "Medicine",
21       "Psychology", "Language", "Culture",
22       "Relationships", "Social Media", "News",
23       "Shopping", "Transportation",
24       "Architecture", "Design", "Gardening",
25       "Hobbies", "Humor", "Literature",
26       "Philosophy", "Photography",
27       "Writing", "Other"])
28  combo1.grid(column=1, row=0, padx=10, pady=5)
29  combo1.set("Holidays")
30
31
32  # Button to submit the details
33  submit_btn = ttk.Button(app, text="Submit",
34                  command=submit)
35  submit_btn.grid(column=0, row=3, padx=10, pady=20)
```

```
36
37   # Button to submit the details
38   create_book_btn = ttk.Button(app,
39      text="Create Book", command=batch_submit)
40   create_book_btn.grid(column=2, row=3, padx=10, pady=20)
41
42   # make it scrollable
43   # Create a Scrollbar widget
44   scrollbar = tk.Scrollbar(app)
45   scrollbar.grid(row=4, column=3, sticky='ns')
46
47   # Text widget to display results
48   result_text = tk.Text(app, width=50, height=10,
49                         wrap=tk.WORD,
50                         yscrollcommand=scrollbar.set)
51   result_text.grid(column=0, row=4, rowspan=1,
52                    columnspan=4, padx=10, pady=10)
53   result_text.config(state="disabled")
54   # result_text.pack(expand=True, fill=tk.BOTH)
55
56   image_holder = tk.Label(app)
57   image_holder.grid(column=0, row=5, columnspan=2,
58                     padx=10, pady=10)
59
60   puzzle_holder = tk.Label(app)
61   puzzle_holder.grid(column=5, row=0, rowspan=7,
62                      padx=2, pady=2)
63
64   label_key_title = ttk.Label(app,
65                               text="Puzzle Words")
66   label_key_title.grid(column=5, row=6, padx=10,
67                        pady=5)
68
69   label_puzzle_words = ttk.Label(app, text="")
70   label_puzzle_words.grid(column=5, row=7,
```

```
71                              padx=10, pady=10)
72
73   # Button to submit the details
74   create_pdf_btn = ttk.Button(
75       app, text="Create Pdf",
76       command=lambda:
77         create_pdf(label_puzzle_words['text']))
78   create_pdf_btn.grid(column=1, row=3, padx=10, pady=20)
79
80   scrollbar.config(command=result_text.yview)
81
82
83   # Link the scrollbar to the text widget
84   # (so the scrollbar knows how to scroll
85   # the text widget)
86
87
88   app.mainloop()
```

This new layout produces the following application screen:

Figure 37. Newly laid out UI

Let's press the "Create Book" button and see what happens. It will take a little bit of time to generate the book on Holidays, but when all is said and done you'll have a 10-page puzzle book! Here is a sample page from our generated Holiday-themed book:

```
K  T  Z  C  U  E  S  J  R  K  B  J  M
N  F  X  Z  T  N  T  W  I  E  S  K  J
J  A  P  D  T  O  F  E  Z  Z  A  Q  V
F  T  T  I  P  I  J  S  F  I  N  T  D
G  T  F  E  A  T  H  E  R  S  E  K  W
U  U  D  O  S  I  K  B  K  Z  W  S  J
T  E  F  M  W  D  W  P  Q  D  O  Z  A
Q  S  V  N  S  A  U  T  Q  G  R  Q  Z
W  D  W  K  L  R  X  A  Y  U  L  Y  Z
Q  A  D  E  P  T  L  H  C  W  E  F  E
E  Y  I  L  E  D  A  R  A  P  A  E  M
P  U  E  N  S  M  A  W  Z  R  N  Y  N
B  R  A  S  S  B  A  N  D  N  S  F  G
```

NEWORLEANS, FATTUESDAY, TRADITION, BRASSBAND, FEATHERS,
PARADE, PURPLE, QUEEN, JAZZ, FETE

Figure 38. One Page from the Holiday Puzzle Book

Conclusion

In summary, producing a PDF word search book by employing
ChatGPT to generate topics and word lists is the next horizon of
game development. We have accomplished this using Python's
powerful puzzle creation and assembly to create a PDF book using
ReportLab. This approach streamlines the production of diverse

and engaging content and provides a unique value proposition for puzzle enthusiasts. Now that we've figured out how to generate a fully viable product, you may want to consider selling what you created! For monetization, a strategic move would be to leverage platforms like Amazon's Kindle Direct Publishing (KDP) and Lean-Pub. Amazon's KDP allows for straightforward self-publishing, providing access to a vast audience of Amazon customers world-wide. You can set your price, receive royalties from every purchase, and retain control over your rights. With Amazon's extensive reach, your word search book can gain visibility, enhancing its sales potential. On the other hand, LeanPub offers a platform specifically designed for authors, where you can publish iteratively, engaging with readers and receiving feedback that enables you to continuously refine the book. LeanPub also provides favorable royalty rates and enables you to publish not only eBooks but also print versions. Starting with a competitive price point and perhaps offering initial discounts or bundles can stimulate initial sales. Utilizing social media and other digital marketing strategies to promote the book across different platforms can further boost visibility and sales. Remember to consider the legal and ethical aspects, securing the necessary rights for selling content generated through AI and adhering to each platform's policies and guidelines.

Appendix

Request for Review

We hope you enjoyed exploring the ChatGPT applications in this book. Your feedback makes a world of difference! If 'Crafting Applications with ChatGPT API' provided value to you, kindly take a moment to share your experience with a review. Your endorsement will not only contribute to the insights gained but also guide fellow enthusiasts in their pursuit of mastering the ChatGPT API. Please drop a review today at the link below:

https://www.amazon.com/Crafting-Applications-ChatGPT-API-Python/dp/B0CHL7H186

Source Code

The source code for all the books projects——the storytelling app, the translation app and the recipe creating website——are all located in github. Feel free to clone the git repository here and run the applications. There may be some setup to do such as installing Python libraries. Instructions for Python library installations are spelled out in each chapter.

https://github.com/microgold/ChatGPTAPIBook

Python Concepts needed for this Book

We don't use much advanced Python in this book. Below are the Python language constructs you'll need to brush up on in order to follow the examples in this book.

Imports: The Entryway to Python's Toolset

In Python, an import allows you to bring in pre-existing functions, classes, or variables from another script or library, making them available for use in your program.

```
1   import math
2   print(math.sqrt(16))   # This will print "4.0"
```

To keep things organized, you can also import specific functions. In the code below, we import the sqrt function from the math library:

```
1   from math import sqrt
2   print(sqrt(16))   # This will also print "4.0"
```

Variable Assignment in Python

In Python, variables do not need explicit declaration to reserve memory space. The declaration happens automatically when you assign a value to a variable. The equal sign (=) is used to assign values to variables.

```
1   # Assigning a value to a variable
2   my_variable = 10
3   name = "Alice"
4   pi = 3.141592653589793
```

In the above example:

- my_variable is assigned an integer value of 10.
- name is assigned a string value of "Alice".
- pi is assigned a floating-point value of approximately 3.141592653589793.

Python's Scope: Focusing on Variable Visibility"

Variable scope determines the part of the program where a variable can be accessed. The basic scopes of variables in Python are:

1. **Local Scope** (Local variables)
2. **Enclosing Scope** (variables in the nearest enclosing scope of nested functions)
3. **Global Scope** (Global variables)
4. **Built-in Scope** (Names in the pre-defined built-ins module)

1. Local Scope:

Variables defined inside a function are said to have a local scope. They can only be accessed within that function, not outside.

```
1   def local_example():
2       local_variable = "I'm local"
3       print(local_variable)
4
5   local_example()   # Prints: I'm local
6   # print(local_variable)   # Uncommenting this
7                              # will raise an error
```

2. Enclosing Scope:

In the case of nested functions, a variable in the outer function is accessible to the inner function but not vice-versa.

```
1   def outer_function():
2       outer_variable = "I'm in the outer function"
3
4       def inner_function():
5           print(outer_variable)
6
7       inner_function()   # This will print: I'm
8                          # in the outer function
9
10  outer_function()
```

3. Global Scope:

Variables declared outside all functions are said to be in the global scope. They can be accessed throughout the program body by all functions, provided we tell Python we intend to refer to the global version of the variable.

```
1   global_variable = "I'm global"
2
3   def function_example():
4       print(global_variable)   # This will print: I'm global
5
6   function_example()
```

To modify a global variable inside a function, you must use the global keyword.

```
1   counter = 0
2
3   def increment_counter():
4       global counter
5       counter += 1
6
7   increment_counter()
8   print(counter)   # Prints: 1
```

4. Built-in Scope:

These are names that are always available in the namespace. For instance, functions like print(), id(), and datatypes like int, float are part of the built-in scope.

Lists: Your Flexible Friends

Lists in Python are versatile and can store an ordered collection of items, which might be of any type. Below we create a list of fruits and add a date to it.

```
1   fruits = ["apple", "banana", "cherry"]
2   fruits.append("date")
3   print(fruits)  # ['apple', 'banana', 'cherry', 'date']
```

To access a list item, refer to its index:

```
1   print(fruits[0])  # 'apple'
```

Dictionaries: An Open Book

In Python, a dictionary is an unordered collection that stores data as key:value pairs. Unlike data structures that hold just one value per element, dictionaries allow us to map unique keys, which can be of any immutable type (like strings, numbers, or tuples), to values that can be of any type and may repeat.

The primary characteristics of dictionaries are:

1. **Unordered**: The items in dictionaries are stored in no particular order.
2. **Mutable**: Dictionaries can be modified after creation.
3. **Indexed by keys**: Items in dictionaries can't be accessed by their position, but instead by their key.

Reading Values from Dictionaries:

To access a value in a dictionary, you reference the key:

```
1  # Defining a dictionary
2  person = {
3      "name": "Alice",
4      "age": 30,
5      "city": "New York"
6  }
7
8  # Accessing a value using its key
9  print(person["name"])  # Outputs: Alice
```

You can also use the get() method, which provides a way to set a default value if the key doesn't exist:

```
1  print(person.get("name"))  # Outputs: Alice
2  print(person.get("country", "USA"))  # Outputs: USA
3                                       #(default value,
4                                       # because 'country'
5                                       #key isn't in the
6                                       # dictionary)
```

Checking if a Key Exists:

Before accessing a key, it's often good to check if it exists in the dictionary to prevent errors:

```
1  if "name" in person:
2      print(f"Name is {person['name']}")
3  else:
4      print("Name not found")
```

Iterating Through a Dictionary:

To iterate through the keys and values in a dictionary, you can use a for loop:

```
1  for key, value in person.items():
2      print(f"{key}: {value}")
```

Tuples: The Immutable Cousin of Lists

Tuples are similar to lists, but their values can't be modified after assignment. They're useful for storing data that shouldn't be altered.

```
1  coordinates = (4.0, 5.0)
```

Tuples are also are useful when you want to return more than one value from a function.

```
1  def rectangle_properties(length, width):
2      area = length * width
3      perimeter = 2 * (length + width)
4
5      # Return both area and perimeter as a tuple
6      return (area, perimeter)
```

Functions: Reusable Code Blocks

Functions are blocks of reusable code. They execute when called by name, and can take parameters and return data. We use them throughout our code examples in order to make the sample code more readable and reusable.

```
1  def greet(name):
2      return f"Hello, {name}!"
3
4  print(greet("Alice"))  # Hello, Alice!
```

Decisions with Conditional Statements

Using if, elif, and else, you can run different blocks of code based on certain conditions:

```
1  def check_number(number):
2      if number > 0:
3          return "Positive"
4      elif number < 0:
5          return "Negative"
6      else:
7          return "Zero"
8
9  print(check_number(5))  # Positive
```

Loops: Iterating with Style

Two main types of loops exist in Python: for and while. for loops are typically used when the number of iterations is known:

for loop

```
1   fruits = ["apple", "banana", "cherry", "date",
2              "elderberry"]
3
4   for fruit in fruits:
5       print(fruit)
```

Output:

```
1   apple
2   banana
3   cherry
4   date
5   elderberry
```

while loop

while loops, on the other hand, are used when the number of iterations is unknown:

```
1   count = 3
2   while count > 0:
3       print(count)
4       count -= 1
```

The output of the provided Python code is:

```
1   3
2   2
3   1
```

The loop starts with count equal to 3. In each iteration of the loop, the value of count is printed, and then it is decremented by 1. The loop continues as long as count is greater than 0.

Wrapping Up

These fundamental Python concepts lay the groundwork for leveraging the power of the ChatGPT API and building robust applications. As we progressed through the book, you saw these concepts come to life in real-world scenarios, providing a hands-on approach to learning and implementation.

Message Structure

The OpenAI ChatCompletion has a particular message structure it expects for the request. Here is a rundown of the details of that message.

Roles in a Message

The following roles are utilized by the API: "system", "user", and "assistant".

system: This role typically provides high-level instructions for the conversation. For example, a system message might set the behavior of the assistant at the beginning of a conversation: {"role": "system", "content": "You are a helpful assistant."}.

user: Represents the end user or developer input in the conversation. It's the query or question that the model responds to: {"role": "user", "content": "Tell me a joke."}.

assistant: Represents the model's response in the conversation. When you receive a reply from the API, messages with the assistant role contain the model's output: {"role": "assistant", "content": "Why did the chicken cross the road? To get to the other side!"}.

If you want OpenAI to act a certain specific way in the conversation, you can use the system role in your message:

Content in a Message

The content is the meat of the prompt. It is here you want to craft your prompt to implement your application.

Example Message

```
1   messages = [
2       {
3           "role": "system",
4           "content": "You are a writer who responds in
5                       the style of Edgar Allan Poe."
6       },
7       {
8           "role": "user",
9           "content": "Write me a very short poem
10                      about a sad ghost"
11      }
12  ]
```

Getting Token Usage

You can also extract token usage from the response of the API call to track how many tokens you used up.

```
1  token_dictionary = {
2      'prompt_tokens':response['usage']
3      ['prompt_tokens'],
4      'completion_tokens':response['usage']
5      ['completion_tokens'],
6      'total_tokens':response['usage']
7      ['total_tokens'],
8  }
```

www.ingramcontent.com/pod-product-compliance
Lightning Source LLC
La Vergne TN
LVHW051239050326
832903LV00028B/2474